Advanced Scrum Case Studies

Real-World Situations and How to Address Them

Frederik M. Fowler

Advanced Scrum Case Studies

ISBN-13 978-1-7371716-1-4

Library of Congress Control Number: 2021910826

Distributed to the book trade worldwide by Silicon Valley Scrum Press, 201 Spear St., Suite 1100, San Francisco, CA 94105; phone, 1-408-505-2813; e-mail ffowler@siliconvalleyscrum.com

Dedication

This book is dedicated to the memory of
Miles Walsh
who first taught me about teams and teamwork.

Table of Contents

- Part I: Problems of Scrum Team Organization, Cross-Functionality, and Self-Management 21
    - Case 1: An Agile Transformation, Started from Scratch 23
    - Case 2: Big-Data Uncertainties 35
    - Case 3: Coders and Testers in Different Locations 47
    - Case 4: Company-Standard Story Points 59
    - Case 5: Database Dependencies 71
    - Case 6: Expanding Offshore 81
    - Case 7: The Java Nazi 93
    - Case 8: Organizing 75 New Developers 105
- Part II : Problems of Management and Product Ownership 115
    - Case 9: Road Map Worries 117
    - Case 10: Fixed-Price Contracts 129
    - Case 11: Dealing with the Director of Engineering 141
    - Case 12: Monitoring Work-from-Home Developers 153
    - Case 13: Coaching an Aggressive Senior Product Owner 163
    - Case 14: Coaching a Spineless Product Owner 173
    - Case 15: Dealing with Unhappy Stakeholders 183
- Summary 195
- Index 199

About the Author

Fred Fowler has been developing software in Silicon Valley for more than 35 years and has been using the Scrum framework since 2006. He is one of only about 50 individuals in the United States who holds the prestigious "Professional Scrum Master Level III" (PSM III) certification awarded by Scrum.org. In 2013, he left his post as VP and CIO of a Silicon Valley 150 company to devote his time to teaching and coaching Scrum/Agile. Since then, he has helped start-ups, not-for-profits, and Fortune 500 organizations, teaching more than 300 people in the United States, India, China, and Central America.

In 2019, he published his first book, *Navigating Hybrid Scrum Environments* (New York: Apress, 2019)

More information is available at https://www.SiliconValleyScrum.com.

Acknowledgments

I wish to thank the many people who participated in the *Advanced Scrum Case Study* discussions over the past six years.

They are too numerous to name individually, but some of the more significant contributors were Jim Schibler, Lauren Smith, Arnel Guanlao, Hanu Molineri, Shruti Bettapour, Michael Combest, David Posey, and Larry Apke.

I would also like to thank Audrey Doyle for editing this book. She provided an invaluable backstop to catch my various grammatical, punctuation, and capitalization mistakes

Foreword

by Larry Apke

I first became aware of Fred Fowler sometime in the beginning of 2015. I had recently taken a position as an Agile Coach in the San Francisco Bay Area and wanted to make connections with the local Agile community. Fred is someone who is easily noticed. It is not that he is bombastic or showy. In fact, he is the opposite. What I most recall about Fred is that he has what I would loosely describe as "presence"—quiet confidence yet commanding ease. I am glad to have met Fred back then, because now, more than six years later, I count him not simply as an astute mentor and a patient and understanding colleague, but as my friend.

Over the past half dozen years, Fred and I have spent a good deal of time together, talking about Agile, swapping stories, and supporting each other's various projects. It is through his support that I was able to create a series of lectures that eventually became my life's passion; this would not have been possible without Fred's influence. For my part, I have tried to repay the favor. Around the time Fred and I met, Fred started his popular meetup group, Silicon Valley Professional Scrum. I joined this group with some regularity. It was through this group that I learned about Fred's Agile Case Studies, some of the more popular of which are presented in this book.

Fred's case study sessions are amazing. The ability to present real-life scenarios, and challenge fellow Agilists to critically examine them and discuss possible solutions vis-à-vis Agile and Scrum, allows participants to flex their Agile muscles in a way that most training does not. Participants are highly engaged when they are presenting and discussing these scenarios. This is certainly one way the case studies in this excellent book can be used: as discussion prompts for Agile meetups and gatherings. This book is worth buying for that reason alone.

But this book is much more than that. Agilists often speak of Agile as being a mindset. Sometimes, more important than the answers provided is the ability to follow the thought process. Throughout the book, Fred presents the conclusions his meetup groups reached, so the reader is privy to the problems as well as the thought processes behind the solutions.

My firsthand knowledge of the efficacy of these scenarios is not limited to Fred's meetup. Part of my Agile journey has led me to create and run a nonprofit that teaches unemployed individuals around the world Agile and Scrum for free. More than 1,000 people have attended my Agile MBA class since I started teaching it around the same time Fred started his meetup. Over the years, we have added Fred's scenarios to our Friday discussion groups. This not only helps my students gain a greater understanding of how to apply Agile and Scrum to real-life situations, it has proven to be the most popular part of these weekly sessions.

You may not have the good fortune, as I do, to know Fred personally. But as you read this compilation of real-life "war stories" and Agile-related scenarios, you will certainly come to know Fred well. What is more, I believe you will become as drawn to his storytelling ability as I was, and continue to be.

Larry Apke
Chief Agile Officer
The Job Hackers
Author of Understanding The Agile Manifesto: A Brief & Bold Guide to Agile *and* Managers from Hell, The PMO is Dead, and Other Agile Stories.

Introduction

In the summer of 2015, I formed a meetup group called Silicon Valley Professional Scrum. I had been practicing Scrum for about 10 years and teaching Scrum classes for about a year. I wanted to form a community around the Scrum framework so that members could trade notes about some of the finer points of using this tool set.

It turned out that many other people wanted this as well. Membership in the group grew quickly, to the point where it now comprises more than 2,000 “Scrumptious People.” They come from all parts of the United States and from all around the world.

Shortly after forming the group, I initiated a discussion of Scrum and Agile case studies. At regular intervals, I would publish a case concerning a problematic situation or scenario. Interested people would sign up and participate in a discussion of the case, looking at it with the Scrum framework in mind and talking about how to address the challenge it presented.

Participants (myself included) found the discussions to be very helpful in understanding not only the various facets of the Scrum framework, but also how to apply the framework in real-world situations. The format of the case was always the same: “Here is a problem situation. As a Scrum framework or Agile professional, how would you deal with it?” We always found a way to deal with the challenges. The discussions that led us to the solutions were informative, educational, and very interesting.

Those case study discussions still take place today. Once every two weeks we publish a new case and have a new discussion. The discussions are online, which provides safety in a COVID-19–

ravaged world but also gives people the opportunity to take part no matter where they are located. Whereas the first case study discussion occurred in my classroom in Silicon Valley and about 15 local people attended, the latest one took place online and included people from as far away as Kathmandu. The reach of Silicon Valley Professional Scrum is now global.

A few years after I started the meetup group, I began to keep records of the cases we discussed. I now have more than 60 cases on file. Every two weeks we add another one to the list. Some of them come from my own experiences and some come from submissions by other members of the group. All of them represent real challenges that real people have faced.

I usually hide details or combine different events together to protect those who were involved. Each case describes a serious problem that an organization faced. To allow each situation to be discussed freely, I make efforts to hide the identity of the organization and its members. Just like the classic television series *Dragnet*, I can say the events depicted are true, and the names have been changed to protect the innocent.

For this book, I selected 15 of the cases I have on file. They are representative of the breadth of the subjects we have covered in our discussions. The topics are as follows:

Problems of Scrum Team Organization, Cross-Functionality, and Self-Management

- Case 1: An Agile Transformation, Started from Scratch
- Case 2: Big-Data Uncertainties
- Case 3: Coders and Testers in Different Locations
- Case 4: Company-Standard Story Points
- Case 5: Database Dependencies
- Case 6: Expanding Offshore
- Case 7: The Java Nazi
- Case 8: Organizing 75 New Developers

Problems of Management and Product Ownership

- Case 9: Road Map Worries
- Case 10: Fixed-Price Contracts
- Case 11: Dealing with the Director of Engineering
- Case 12: Monitoring Work-from-Home Developers
- Case 13: Coaching an Aggressive Senior Product Owner
- Case 14: Coaching a Spineless Product Owner
- Case 15: Dealing with Unhappy Stakeholders

For each case, I outline the problem, give any necessary background information, and then apply the tools of the Scrum framework to figure out a course of action. The solutions I present mirror the conclusions reached in the original meetup discussions.

As the title of this book suggests, *Advanced Scrum Case Studies* is not aimed at Scrum beginners. It is assumed that you already know the basics when it comes to the Scrum framework. The discussions this book is based on were intended to help people advance their existing understanding of Scrum. Many of the participants in those discussions over the years have gone on to earn advanced Scrum certifications (such as CSP or PSM II). They all say the case study discussions they participated in were excellent preparation for earning those advanced certifications.

People with no Scrum background are advised to learn the basics before reading the cases in this book. One way to do so is to read my first book, *Navigating Hybrid Scrum Environments* (New York: Apress, 2019). Despite its title, the book contains a detailed and thorough explanation of the Scrum framework. It is taken from the classroom material I have used to teach Scrum to new Scrum Masters, Product Owners, and Scrum developers.

As I noted earlier, this book contains 15 cases, but I currently have enough cases on file to fill three more books like this one. In addition, every two weeks another case is added to the list. So, depending on the amount of interest readers show in *Advanced*

Scrum Case Studies, it might be followed shortly by *More Advanced Scrum Case Studies*, *Even More Advanced Scrum Case Studies*, and *Even Even More Advanced Scrum Case Studies*. We'll see.

I invite you to join the Silicon Valley Professional Scrum meetup group and participate in the discussions that produced this book. If you have faced (or are currently facing) a challenge similar to the ones listed here, I invite you to submit it as a case for future discussion. If you do, you may find a community of Scrum framework practitioners discussing your problem and offering solutions.

As Ken Schwaber, co-author of *The Scrum Guide*, would say, "Scrum on!"

--Fred Fowler, DS, PSM III
San Francisco, California
April 2021

A Quick Refresher

This book is intended for people who are already familiar with the Scrum framework and its components.

Having said that, here is a brief review of the Scrum framework: its roles, artifacts, and events.

Roles

The Scrum framework defines three roles. These roles identify sets of responsibilities accepted by the individuals playing these roles.

Developers

Developers are technicians who accept responsibility for creating a product. They form a development team within an overall Scrum Team.

The development team must have all the skills necessary to create the product by itself, with no help from outside the team. The development team must also manage itself, making all decisions as to how the product is to be created.

Product Owner

A Product Owner is a business professional who accepts responsibility for maximizing the value of a product. He or she does so by identifying valuable improvements for the development team to make to the product. The Product Owner invests the development team's time and effort to improve the product. The Product Owner's relative success can be measured through the return on those investments (ROI).

Scrum Master

A Scrum Master is a teacher and coach who accepts responsibility for making sure a Scrum Team uses the Scrum framework properly. He or she teaches and coaches the Product Owner and the developers on how to live up to their responsibilities and collaborate as a team.

Together, the Product Owner, development team, and Scrum Master form a Scrum Team.

Artifacts

The Scrum framework identifies three artifacts used to provide transparency for Scrum Teams to inspect.

Product Backlog

A Product Backlog is an ordered list of the improvements to be made to a product. This list is owned and maintained by the Product Owner. All development work is based on this list.

Sprint Backlog

A Sprint Backlog is a plan for achieving the goal of a Sprint (I discuss Sprints in more detail in the "Events" section).

At the beginning of each Sprint, a goal for it is negotiated between the Product Owner and the development team. Together, they agree on implementing a set of Product Backlog items that are expected to achieve the goal. Once the goal and the Product Backlog items have been agreed to, the development team creates a work plan. This work plan is referred to as the Sprint Backlog.

Increment

An Increment is a finished and "done" improvement to a product. Every Sprint must produce at least one Increment.

Events

The Scrum framework identifies five events. Each event is a formal opportunity for inspection and adaptation.

The Sprint

The Sprint is a time-boxed event for inspecting and adapting the product. It is a container for all the other events within the Scrum framework.

The Sprint Planning Meeting

The Sprint Planning meeting is a time-boxed event for negotiating the goal and scope of a Sprint. The Product Owner and the development team discuss and agree on a goal for the upcoming Sprint's work. Then they negotiate a set of Product Backlog items to be included. Finally, the development team creates a work plan for the Sprint. This work plan is called the Sprint Backlog.

During the Sprint Planning meeting, the Product Backlog is inspected and the Sprint Backlog is adapted.

The Daily Scrum

The Daily Scrum is a daily, 15-minute meeting of the development team. The members of the team inspect the status of their work and adapt their work plan to cover any unexpected issues.

The Sprint Review

At the end of each Sprint, the Scrum Team plus any guests the Product Owner invites get together to review the newly created version of the product. This new version includes the old features plus the new ones created during the Sprint. The new version is inspected, and new items are added to the Product Backlog if any are identified during the inspection.

The Sprint Retrospective

After the Sprint Review, the Scrum Team meets to discuss the things that went well, the things that did not go well, and any lessons learned. Through this self-inspection, the team members adapt how they face challenges and work together.

Agile Coach

While not a formal role within the Scrum framework, an Agile Coach is a teacher and coach just as the Scrum Master is. The difference lies in the audience for the teaching and coaching that is performed.

A Scrum Master's audience is one or more Scrum Teams. The Scrum Master helps Scrum Teams use the Scrum framework effectively.

An Agile Coach's audience is the organization as a whole. The Agile Coach teaches the organization (and especially its managers) how the Scrum framework works, what to expect from it, and how to support it effectively.

Part I:

Problems of Scrum Team Organization, Cross-Functionality, and Self-Management

Case 1:

An Agile Transformation, Started from Scratch

You are an Agile Coach. You have been retained by a new chief information officer (CIO) for an organization that wants to "go Agile." The CIO joined the organization to turn around a failing software development effort. You have been hired to rescue the project and spearhead a comprehensive Agile transformation of the software group.

The organization is a longtime player in a traditional (not high-tech) business. It develops software for internal use and for managing its various business processes. The organization attempted to re-platform its software to move away from its legacy big iron and toward cloud-based, scalable systems. It is partway through a waterfall project to replace a key component of its software portfolio.

It is widely perceived within the organization that this project has failed. All the managers associated with it have been fired.

The new CIO has given you carte blanche to transform the project and the organization along Agile lines. The CIO expects to see measurable improvements within 90 days and continuing improvements on a quarterly basis.

Your assignment:

1. Analyze this situation vis-à-vis the Scrum framework.
2. Outline a plan for accomplishing the transformation and describe the initial steps in detail.

This case study depicts a situation in which an Agile Coach is positioned to facilitate an Agile transformation starting from a clean slate. The old approach for developing complicated software was attempted and everyone agrees the attempt was a failure. Both management and the rest of the organization are now open to a new approach.

As an Agile Coach, you have full discretionary power to change things. At the same time, you cannot afford any missteps. You have been given only one chance to transform the organization. If anything is bungled, you will likely be terminated immediately. After the big, embarrassing failure of the previous waterfall project, the organization and its shareholders have no patience for mistakes.

Initial Analysis

Your first action is to try to understand what happened with the initial re-platform attempt: it was deemed a failure and all the managers associated with it lost their jobs. You want to know why.

It turns out that the answer is a simple one. The organization hired a software services firm to undertake the project. The firm brought in almost 100 software engineers to do the work. After a year, a great deal of new software had been written but no new functionality had been finished and delivered. Lots of “pieces” had been created but there had been no real attempt to fit them together. There was almost nothing tangible to show for the 12 months’ worth of time and money that had been spent.

You admire the organization’s top managers for having the courage to call the attempt a failure. You admire them for pulling the plug.

Delivering Value

Clearly, the way to avoid a second failure is to focus on delivering value on a regular basis. After hearing nothing but promises for 12 months, top management want to see real progress. They want to see working software, and see it delivered at a pace that will give them hope and confidence that the new approach will work.

Where to start? The Scrum framework is designed to facilitate the creation of valuable products. It does so by dividing the challenge into two parts. One part is to understand what will be valuable to create. The other part is to figure out how to create it.

The Scrum framework defines a role called Product Owner. The Product Owner is accountable for a product and makes decisions designed to maximize its value. The Product Owner makes all the decisions about “what to create.”

The Product Owner “owns” a product, but what is a product? A product is something that can be produced and that has an objectively measurable value. The value must be measurable, because the Product Owner’s job is to maximize the product’s value. It is impossible to maximize something that cannot be measured.

So, what is the product in this case? The goal of the initiative is to replace all the legacy software the organization uses to conduct its business. Many different functions are used to handle different aspects of the work. Many of those functions have values that can be measured. Should there be just one product, or many?

After some investigation, you determine that several areas of work have measurable value and can stand alone. For example, there is a warehousing activity the organization spent a great deal of resources to support. There is also a sales effort that is very important. Both need software to support them.

The value of the warehouse support software can be measured by the cost of warehousing the organization's goods. If a software improvement reduces that cost, the value of the improvement will be the amount of the cost reduction.

The value of the sales support software can be measured by its impact on the organization's revenue. If an improvement increases the organization's sales, the value of the improvement will be the increase in sales revenue.

The value of the warehouse function does not depend on the value of the sales support function, and vice versa. Furthermore, decisions about how to optimize the value of one function have little to do with how to optimize the value of the other. It makes sense to classify these as separate products with separate people responsible for maximizing their value.

Linking Products with Product Owners

The computer services firm that initially worked on the project used a group of business analysts to develop technical specifications for the coders to follow. The analysts spent a great deal of time interviewing various people in the organization to determine what was needed. After several months, they produced a specification and a project plan designed to deliver the system they envisioned.

One reason no actual functionality was put into use after 12 months was that the organization's middle managers did not feel the business analysts who created the plan truly understood how the organization worked. The analysts created complicated processes and procedures to deal with simple situations, and omitted several critical functions entirely. None of these issues became apparent until the coders reported that the functions were ready to test. Functions that were submitted for acceptance testing were rejected, not because of mistakes made in coding them but because of mistakes made when designing them.

In the end, the organization realized the business analysts who created the specification and the plan were not the right people to do so. Warehouse support functions should not be designed by business analysts; they should be designed by warehouse people. Likewise, sales support functions should not be designed by business analysts; they should be designed by sales and sales support people. The business analysts could write comprehensive specifications and a detailed project plan. The mistake they made was selecting the wrong problems for the coders to solve.

The Scrum framework puts the responsibility for identifying the right problems to solve on the shoulders of the Product Owner. The Product Owner's main responsibility is to create and maintain a sequenced list of problems for the development team to solve. This list is called the Product Backlog. Each item in the list identifies something valuable for the development team to work on. The item is not "finished" until the value is realized.

There is a common misunderstanding that the role of Product Owner is a technical role and should be held by someone with a technical background. It is not. The Product Owner's job is to understand and make choices about the business problems to be solved. The Product Owner is concerned with what to do, not how to do it. The technology involved is irrelevant to the choices a Product Owner makes.

The person making decisions about which warehouse support problems should be solved should be the person who owns the warehouse function. Likewise, the person making decisions about which sales support problems should be solved should be the person responsible for the sales support function.

After classifying the various functions of the organization as Scrum framework products, the middle managers in charge of these business functions became the Product Owners for these products.

Creating the Product Backlog

A Product Owner's job is to create and maintain a Product Backlog, which is a list of problems to solve. These problems might imply new capabilities to create or old capabilities to change. Each one should have a business purpose behind it. Also, each one should have a measurable value associated with it.

A common misconception is that a Product Backlog item contains a list of technical specifications for the development team to follow. This is not true. A Product Backlog item should present a challenge for the technical people on the development team to address. To meet the challenge, the developers should create and follow their own plan and their own technical specifications. The test of their success lies not in how well they follow instructions, but in how well their solution addresses the problem the Product Backlog item poses.

Creating User Stories

A useful tool for Product Owners to use when creating Product Backlog items is the user story. A user story describes, in a nontechnical way, the needs of a particular user from that user's point of view and explains the reason for that need.

The user story format has the following main components.

- Who: Which user (or user role) has the need?
- What: What is the description of the need?
- Why: What is the reason the need exists?

So, for the following user story:

"As a warehouse worker, I need to be able to look up the location of an item quickly so that I can pick it efficiently."

- The user with the need is a warehouse worker (who).
- The need is to be able to look up item locations quickly (what).
- The reason for the need is that the user needs to "pick" items efficiently (why).

The user story format also helps the Product Owner gauge how valuable it would be to solve the problem. By identifying the user (or user role) that is affected, the Product Owner can understand how many people might be helped. By identifying the reason the need exists, the Product Owner can evaluate how significant the help can be to the organization and its operations. If, for example, the organization had 10 warehouse workers, 50 products, and 100 orders per day, it might not make sense to create a software-based way to find the items; a paper map would do. However, if the organization had 200 warehouse workers, 10,000 products, and 3,000 orders per day, it might make sense to spend a great deal of effort to make it easier to locate things.

Affinity Mapping

Another tool that can be useful for the Product Owner is the affinity mapping technique for assigning values to stories. An affinity map is not used to assign absolute values to stories. It is used to figure out the relative values of stories in a set.

A Product Owner needs to prioritize the items in the Product Backlog such that the development team is always working on the most valuable items it can at any given time. One way to do this is to compare the estimated values of stories and arrange them accordingly. The first item goes on the list, and the second one goes either above it or below it depending on whether it has more value or less value than the first one. The third item then goes either at the top of the list, at the bottom of the list, or in the middle depending on its value in relation to the two other items. More items are added either above, between, or below the ones already there. When all the Product Backlog items have been added to the list, the items are in descending value sequence.

Ranking items in this way does not require that the actual values of the items be calculated. It is enough just to be able to say that one item is more (or less) valuable than another.

Refining the Product Backlog

So far, the Product Owners have been able to focus on their business needs and create their Product Backlog wish lists without regard to the technical details of how to address those needs. They have focused on "what to do."

The next step is to start engaging the technical people. After the initial Product Backlog has been created, it is time to start asking the question, "How will it all be done?"

To answer this question, the Product Owners must identify the developers who should work on these Product Backlogs.

The organization has a small staff of permanently employed technical people who maintain and run the legacy big iron the organization depends on. Additionally, there are 100 contract software developers who were originally supplied by the computer services firm. The fate of the contractors has not been decided yet. The new CIO discontinued the organization's relationship with the computer services firm but does not want to let the contractors go until she knows whether they will be needed or not.

As the Agile Coach, you suggest to the Product Owners that they review the resumes of all the available technical people (both permanent and contract) to find one or two people who might be knowledgeable about the Product Owners' functional areas. The warehouse support Product Owner might look for a technical person with a background in warehouse systems. The sales support Product Owner might look for a person with a sales support background. The goal is for the Product Owners to find at least one technical person who "speaks their language" and can talk with them.

Each Product Owner then presents the items in the Product Backlog to the technical person. They discuss each item with two goals in mind.

1. Figure out what technical skills might be required to address the problem.
2. Figure out how challenging it might be to solve.

As the required technical skills are identified, each Product Owner asks the technical person to find and/or help recruit people who have those skills. As new people are recruited, they join in the process and identify more needs. Analysis and recruitment continues until all the skill needs are met.

The sizes of the challenges in the Product Backlog items are also evaluated and adjusted if necessary. If an item is of such a general nature that addressing it might take months, the need should be refined so that it is broken into several, more-specific parts. For example, the need "look up an item's location in the warehouse" might be broken into "enter an item identifier into the system without having to use a keyboard," "get visual or auditory directions to follow in the warehouse," and "record the picking of the item without having to use a keyboard." Each need should have a measurable value and should be able to be ranked with the other Product Backlog items.

Once this process is finished, it will have accomplished two very important goals.

1. The Product Backlogs will now contain technically feasible items that have measurable value.
2. Each product will have an identified team of technical people who have the skills necessary to create it.

At this point, the teams have what they need to start their Sprint cycles. The technical people and the Product Owners negotiate and agree on the items to be delivered, the technical people (i.e., the development team) manage themselves to deliver what they agreed to deliver, everyone involved reviews the value delivered, and the cycle starts over again.

The original desire of top management to see progress on a regular basis is served by the Scrum framework and its emphasis on maximizing value. Every Product Backlog item must have value in the eyes of the business (or else it would never be prioritized for implementation). At the end of each Sprint, this added value is made transparent during the Sprint Review. In order to be reviewed, each item must be done and ready to be put to use with no further work required.

One More Set of Decisions Is Needed

So, are you finished at this point? Not quite.

As previously described, the Scrum Product Owner is an investor. He or she invests the time and energy of the team working on the product in order to increase its value.

The Product Owner is empowered to make all decisions about how the skills and talents of the development team will be used. One decision the Product Owner is not in a position to make, though, is how many people he or she may work with compared to the number of those working with other Product Owners. If there are 100 available contractors, which products should get more of them and which should get fewer? Product Owners are accountable for the value of their own products. They cannot be asked to decide whether their products are more or less valuable or important than anyone else's.

There is an important role for top management in this situation. Just as Product Owners are investors, top management must make investment decisions as well. They need to decide how to allocate scarce resources among the different product development efforts. They need to decide whether warehouse support services or sales support services are more important. Once they do, they need to allocate resources to those areas accordingly.

Conclusion

In this situation, the original waterfall project failed for several reasons.

- It attempted to create a comprehensive solution without truly understanding the problem.
- It focused on process rather than results.
- It generated quite a bit of activity but delivered little or no value.

The Scrum framework-based approach addresses these failures.

- It empowers the people most affected by problems to identify and prioritize them.
- It de-emphasizes process in favor of results.
- It delivers tangible value according to a predictable schedule.

You, as the Agile Coach, have achieved the transformation by doing the following:

- Identifying the products correctly
- Identifying Product Owners for them

- Coaching the Product Owners and developers to form Scrum Teams and refine the Product Backlog items effectively
- Using the Sprint cycle to manage development activities
- Showing measurable results at the end of every Sprint

Case 2:

Big-Data Uncertainties

You are a Scrum Master who is new to a company. You are assigned to a team whose task is to maintain and improve a tool used by customers to analyze big data. The tool consists of a front end where users input various control parameters, a processing engine where the big-data store is queried and analyzed, and an output end where results are displayed, printed, transmitted, or e-mailed to various recipients.

The team is large—18 people. Some are proficient in UI tools such as AngularJS. Others are skilled at big-data manipulation tools and algorithms. Still others are expert at report creation and distribution techniques.

The Scrum events do not seem to be working well. The team members are mostly quiet during the Sprint Planning meeting, the Daily Scrum, and the Sprint Retrospective (the team does not hold a Sprint Review).

The Product Owner maintains a Product Backlog of high-level objectives that usually include creating new features. Each Product Backlog Item typically involves a combination of UI work, analytics work, and reporting work. The development team attempts to put sizes on these features using story points, but the results are not viewed as consistent. The team members have a great deal of trouble meeting the forecasts they make in the Sprint Planning meeting.

Your assignment:

1. Analyze the situation vis-à-vis the Scrum framework.

2. Describe a plan of action for improvement.

This case illustrates some of the challenges teams face as they attempt to be both self-managing and cross-functional.

Initial Analysis

As the Scrum Master, you start your work by reviewing the Product Backlog. It contains several items representing features requested by the company's clients. Each feature is specified using the user story format: "As a [type of user], I wish to [use a feature] so that [my need is filled]." The Product Owner has done a good job assigning values to the numerous items in the Product Backlog and sequencing them in an appropriate way. So far, so good.

Some alarm bells start to sound in your head when you participate in the next Sprint Planning meeting. During the meeting, the Product Owner presents the Product Backlog and indicates which items are the most important to finish. The development team members say they will work on the first four or five items on the list, and then use a form of "planning poker" to assign story point values to the items they selected. When that process is finished, the Sprint Planning meeting comes to an end.

Before the actual work begins, the lead UI developer, lead analytics developer, and lead reporting developer meet, and together they break down the selected Product Backlog items and create instructions for the other developers to follow. Then they assign tasks to the various members of the team. Each team member is accountable for completing the tasks he or she has been assigned.

The team holds a 15-minute Daily Scrum every morning. It consists of the UI developers reporting their status to the lead UI developer, followed by the analytics developers reporting their status to the lead analytics developer. If there is time, the reporting developers relate their status to the lead reporting developer, but often the 15-minute time limit is reached before the reporting developers get a chance to share their information. There is some talk about rotating the order of the groups so that everyone gets a chance to speak at least a few days per week. There is not much enthusiasm for such a rotation, though, because many people feel the Daily Scrum is a waste of time anyway.

The three lead developers maintain burn-down charts of their team members' work. Each team member has a separate chart showing pending, in-progress, and completed tasks. Each team member is pressured to bring his or her pending and in-progress tasks to zero by the end of the Sprint.

Applying the Scrum Framework

The Scrum framework requires that Scrum development teams be cross-functional and self-managing. Cross-functional means the development team has the ability to create the product without any help from outside its membership. Cross-functional means that since the team has the ability to create the product, it can accept responsibility for doing so.

Self-managing means the team decides how to create the product, with no direction from outside its membership. Self-managing means that since the team can decide how to manage itself to create the product, it can accept responsibility for doing so.

Both cross-functionality and self-management are necessary for a team to take responsibility for the results it produces. When these two characteristics are present, the team's members cannot point fingers at anyone outside the team if the results are not good. The team has the ability to create the product and can make all the decisions about how to do so. It owns the results it produces. There are no excuses.

In this situation, it appears that the team is both cross-functional and self-managing. The problem seems to be that the team members are not doing a very good job of managing themselves, and they are not taking responsibility for their actions. As the Scrum Master, you decide to coach them to divide the work, break into smaller teams, help one another, and measure their ability to deliver results.

Refining the Product Backlog

During the next Sprint Retrospective, you initiate a broad discussion about how things are working. You ask an open question about what is working well and what is not working well.

One theme that emerges is that no one, other than the three leads, has a clear understanding of what they are trying to accomplish. Each person has been given a list of assignments to complete, but only the lead developers know how the pieces fit together. The other developers never see the finished product the way a user would. They would like to see the big picture and understand how the tasks they have been assigned will help improve the product.

As the Scrum Master, you start asking some questions. You ask whether the team members discuss the Product Backlog items together before accepting them into a Sprint. You also ask whether the developers get a chance to ask questions of the Product Owner to clarify the intent of the Product Backlog items and the kinds of needs they represent.

It turns out that there is very little discussion of the Product Backlog items by the team as a whole. Most of the clarification is done between the Product Owner and the three leads. When the leads are satisfied that they understand a Product Backlog item, they create UX/UI, analytics, and reporting task lists to implement the item.

You then ask whether the other developers would like to be part of the clarification process. You point out that the Scrum framework contains a recommendation that up to 10% of each Sprint be devoted to Product Backlog refinement, a process in which Product Backlog items that will be worked on in future Sprints are discussed. The purpose of Product Backlog refinement is to make sure everyone involved understands the need each Product Backlog item is meant to fill. It also lets the development team as a whole understand how challenging it will be to fill the need and start developing a plan to meet that challenge.

All the junior-level members of the development team announce that they are very interested in participating in Product Backlog refinement. They point out that they could learn a lot by taking part in this discussion and would be better able to put their own tasks into broader context.

As the Scrum Master, you point out that the Scrum framework calls for experimentation. You suggest that the Scrum Team try a full Product Backlog refinement session and see what happens. Rather than speculating about what the result might be, you tell them to "try it and see."

After a short discussion, the Product Owner and the leads agree to invite everyone to the next "clarification" session. You make sure that an adequately sized room is reserved and that everyone is given access to the current Product Backlog before the meeting.

The Refinement Discussion

At the beginning of the meeting, you ask the Product Owner to describe the first item in the Product Backlog. You ask him to discuss what the user story says and why the need it describes is important from the user's point of view. You also ask him to describe aspects of the need that will affect the user's impression of the product, such as how convenient is it for the user to use the new functionality and how quickly it responds to the user's request. Finally, you ask the Product Owner to describe how valuable it would be to the company to fill this need.

You then ask the development team how they would go about filling the need. What new functions would have to be created and what impacts would there be on the product's UX/UI, analytics, and reporting components?

For the first Product Backlog item, it turns out that the need is great and filling it would be very valuable to the company. It also turns out that filling the need only involves some minor tweaks to the user interface, some moderately complicated additions to the analytics layer, and only one new reporting component.

One of the UX/UI developers offers to take care of the user interface, one of the reporting developers volunteers to take care of the new reporting requirement, and two analytics developers volunteer to collaborate on the analytics changes. Together, the four developers consider the size of the challenge to be "small."

The next Product Backlog item is also valuable, but more challenging from a technical point of view. It involves creating a brand-new, consolidated user interface for several existing functions. This will require quite a bit of UX/UI work, with only limited analytics and/or reporting changes.

The UX/UI lead offers to take on this Product Backlog item and asks for help from the other UX/UI people. Three of the junior-level UX/UI developers agree to work with the lead on this Product Backlog item. A junior analytics developer and a junior reporting developer offer to take care of the small changes needed here. Overall, they agree that the size of the challenge is "large."

The next Product Backlog item is a little less valuable but still very important. It involves implementing a completely new way of reporting the results of existing inquiries. Up until now, the reports have been produced on demand. The new functionality involves scheduling reports for automatic generation with variable parameters (e.g., "as of date") and recipient distribution lists. No changes will be needed for the analytics layer, but a very substantial change will be needed for the reporting component. A new user interface will be needed to provide a front end for the new reporting features.

The reporting lead offers to oversee this Product Backlog item but notes that the challenge is too big for one person. She asks for help from the other reporting developers. Three of the junior-level reporting developers agree to join the effort. No analytics changes are needed, but a UX/UI developer volunteers to develop the necessary front end. Together, they agree that the size of the challenge is "large."

The next Product Backlog item involves the analytics layer only. Users have been complaining about the poor response time they experience when making inquiries into the big-data storehouse. They point out that complicated searches can take 20 minutes to return results when similar searches on competitors' platforms are completed in just five minutes. Improving performance will make the product more competitive in the eyes of potential new customers and would therefore be very valuable for the company if it could be accomplished.

The analytics lead offers to take on this need and asks for help from the other analytics developers. Several of them volunteer to join the effort. They agree that the challenge is "very large."

Since this challenge is "very large," you ask whether it might be too large. Should it be broken down into smaller pieces?

After some discussion with the developers, the Product Owner agrees to divide the need into several small needs based on the type of inquiry used. The developers note that different types of inquiries use different underlying mechanisms. If they could work on the different mechanisms one at a time, the challenge of each one would only be "large" and not "very large." The Product Owner notes that some types of inquiries are more important than others and that optimizing the performance of one or two would deliver the lion's share of the value involved.

Discussion of the next few Product Backlog items continues along the lines described above. As the items get less valuable going down the list, you encourage the team not to spend too much time discussing them. It is important to discuss items fully if it is likely they will be included in the next one or two Sprints. The further into the future the items are, the less important it is to try to understand them in detail. Things can and do change; needs can change. A general understanding of less important (and thus less imminent) Product Backlog items is useful, but a detailed understanding is vital for those items that will be worked on next.

You encourage the Product Owner to make note of the sizes the developers placed on the Product Backlog items they refined, and to record the names of the developers who volunteered to work on each one.

The Sprint Planning Meeting

When it is time for the next Sprint Planning meeting, you convene it by asking the Product Owner and the developers to discuss what the objective of the upcoming Sprint should be. They will be working on a number of Product Backlog items, but why will they be doing the work? What overall goal will they be trying to accomplish?

You explain that the Scrum framework calls for the Product Owner and the developers to agree on a Sprint Goal for the work they will do. This goal is a unifying purpose the entire Scrum Team is trying to serve.

After a brief discussion, they all agree that the goal of the Sprint will be to prove that they can work together effectively. They want to prove to themselves that they can take on a series of challenges and deliver real value. Everything they do during the Sprint will be aimed at eliminating the need for excuses. They state the goal in this way: "The goal is to show we can meet the challenges we choose to accept, and deliver more value than it costs to produce that value."

With that goal in mind, the discussion turns to the Product Backlog and its items. Since the items were already discussed in detail during the Product Backlog refinement process, there is very little need to discuss them further.

After a short discussion, everyone agrees that the development team can take on the following items:

- Item 1: Minor tweaks (high value, small size)
- Item 2: UX reorganization (high value, large size)
- Item 3: Reporting enhancements (high value, large size)
- Item 4: Performance enhancement of one type of inquiry (high value, large size)
- Item 5: Another item similar to Item 1 (lower value, small size)

As the Scrum Master, you encourage the developers who volunteered to work on the various items to meet among themselves to determine their work plans. Items 2, 3, and 4 all have groups of developers who have the skills needed to create their respective solutions. The group of developers who volunteered to work on Item 1 also agreed to take on Item 5, since both of them are similar in content and size.

The Daily Scrum

As work progresses, you encourage the teams to meet on a daily basis to understand their status. There is no need, for instance, for the people working on Item 4 (performance enhancement) to meet daily with the people working on Item 3 (reporting enhancements). The Daily Scrum's purpose is to let people ask for and receive help from other team members if they run into trouble. The reporting people cannot help with the analytics work, and vice versa. Each team should hold its own 15-minute daily meeting to make sure it is on track to deliver what it agreed to deliver.

At the same time, it is possible that one team might end up needing help from another team. To deal with that possibility, it makes sense for one or two representatives from each team to come together on a daily basis. Their job would be to bring to light any issues in which one team's challenges might affect another team (or teams). If such an issue is uncovered, the representatives should bring together everyone who is affected to figure out what to do about it.

The Sprint Review

At the end of the Sprint, you encourage the Product Owner and the developers to hold a formal Sprint Review meeting. The purpose of the meeting will be to show what the product can do in its current state. The developers are immediately interested in taking part. They have long complained that they would like to understand the big picture and see the product from the end user's point of view. The Sprint Review would be a valuable opportunity to do so.

You encourage the Product Owner to invite some actual customers to join the review. Several of them are very interested and agree to make the time needed to do so.

On the day of the Sprint Review, the Product Owner welcomes everyone, introduces the team members to the customers, and introduces the customers to the team members. He then demonstrates the new version of the product, briefly going over its older features and discussing its new features in detail. He describes the latest sets of enhancements that have been completed, explaining how they work and the needs they are intended to fill. Then he shows the current Product Backlog and briefly describes the more important items that are to be worked on next.

During the presentation, the customers are invited to make comments and/or ask questions. A number of them do so. Some of them ask for adjustments to the user interface for the newer features. Others ask for new capabilities altogether. Still others note that some existing features have little value from their point of view and wonder why they are included.

The Product Owner asks the customers who suggested new capabilities to estimate the value of the capabilities. He also asks the developers to give a preliminary estimate for whether each capability would be a “small,” “large,” or “very large” challenge to implement. Based on these estimates, the Product Owner chooses to add them to the Product Backlog and adjusts the order of the items in the Product Backlog to reflect the new priorities he feels are appropriate.

The Sprint Retrospective

After the Sprint Review, the entire group meets in a conference room to conduct a Sprint Retrospective. The discussion centers on what worked well and what could have worked better. The team notes that the people working on the two "small" challenges were finished with time to spare, whereas the people working on the reporting enhancements barely finished on time. They decide to try to do a better job of understanding how "large" or "small" challenges really are before they commit to meeting them.

They also agree that having everyone involved in the Product Backlog refinement process was a vast improvement over the way things were done previously. Understanding the needs in the Product Backlog ahead of time and making preliminary choices about how to meet them made the entire process work much better. The goal was "... to show we can meet the challenges we choose to accept, and deliver more value than it costs to produce." That goal was met.

Conclusion

Large Scrum development teams can manage themselves more effectively if they break into smaller teams with specific goals in mind. This case study illustrated the application of a modified "scaled Scrum" approach in which the development team not only managed its work plan but also managed its scaled team structure. The development team was accountable for figuring out the "how" part of the puzzle of delivering value. That included how to divide the work among a group of individual subteams if necessary.

Case 3:

Coders and Testers in Different Locations

You are a Scrum Master and you have been hired to "fix" a Scrum Team. The team is offshore, with a group of coders in India and a group of quality assurance (QA) technicians in Ukraine. You are in Silicon Valley and so is the Product Owner. As far as you can tell, the Product Owner is experienced in the position and knows her job.

The QA technicians operate on a "one Sprint behind" principle, meaning that the work the coders do in Sprint A is tested in Sprint B. There is friction, because once the coders are done with their Sprint work, they move on to new tasks, but the QA process forces them to fix bugs in the old work while they are trying to meet their commitments on the new work.

Your assignment:

1. Analyze this situation vis-à-vis the Scrum framework.

2. Come up with a course of action to take.

This case illustrates some of the challenges involving remote and distributed Scrum development teams.

Initial Analysis

As the Scrum Master, the first question you ask is, "Why are the coders and the QA technicians in different locations?" It turns out that they are separated for cost reasons.

The company's engineering manager decided to have a number of computer service providers bid on different parts of the job. He ultimately felt that having two providers would help him negotiate favorable rates for the workers that were supplied. In the end, a provider in India bid the lowest for the coders and a provider in Ukraine bid the lowest for the QA technicians.

Both providers could have supplied all the necessary people, but the engineering manager didn't want to have a sole source for the technical talent. He divided the contracts so that he could threaten to cut one provider off and use the other if any kind of conflict arose. He uses this leverage to put pressure on the providers to have their people "deliver."

By far, the biggest challenge facing you and the Product Owner has to do with the time difference involved. The time difference between Silicon Valley and India is 12 hours 30 minutes. The time difference between Silicon Valley and Kyiv, the capital of Ukraine, is nine hours. The Internet makes communicating over such distances very inexpensive, but finding a time of day when communicating is practical is very difficult.

The Scrum framework mandates that the development team must be cross-functional and self-managing. For Scrum to work, the members of the development team must work together to select items to deliver and bring them to completion.

As the Scrum Master, you realize that instead of one development team, there are two. Both the India and Ukraine teams manage themselves because they are too far away for the Silicon Valley group to do it.

Unfortunately, neither team is cross-functional. A Scrum framework development team must be able to create its product with no help from the outside. The team in India can do part of the work but not all of it. Likewise, the team in Ukraine cannot deliver a "done" Increment by itself. Neither team can accept accountability for delivering results. In fact, no one in this scenario is accountable for delivering results.

You realize that the key to "fixing" the Scrum Team is to take these two groups and help them come together. They need to think and act like a single team. They should not think of themselves as the "coders" or the "QA techs." They should think of themselves as professionals who have the ability to create a product and who accept accountability for doing so.

Breaking Down Barriers

You realize that a great deal of coaching is needed; you must work with both teams to get them to interact with each other. You also realize that you cannot coach them remotely. As the Manifesto for Agile Software Development states: "The most efficient and effective method of conveying information to and within a development team is face-to-face conversation." You must get out of Silicon Valley and spend time in India and Ukraine.

You approach the engineering manager and ask for travel funds. At first, the engineering manager is suspicious and is reluctant to approve the travel. You point out that the need for the travel is a direct result of the engineering manager's choice to use two separate providers to source the technical talent being used. If the engineering manager wishes to reap any benefit from the low hourly rates he has negotiated with the providers, the teams must become productive. You state that you cannot help unless you can talk with the developers face-to-face.

In addition to asking for the means to travel to the offshore locations, you ask for funds to allow the teams in India and Ukraine to visit each other. They need to be able to talk and work with each other on a face-to-face basis as well.

In the end, the travel funds are approved.

Meeting Face-to-Face

When you arrive at the location in India, you introduce yourself to the team of coders working there. They work in a large, modern building that houses hundreds of technical people working on dozens of different projects for dozens of different clients, including big names such as Google, Oracle, and Cisco Systems. Your company is very small in comparison. Your team of coders has only six members.

As you get to know the coders, you learn that the team includes two very experienced people, two intermediate people, and two relative beginners. The provider allocated these people to your company's project with the expectation that the senior coders would lead the effort. The provider did not expect the junior coders to contribute very much. It was expected that the senior and intermediate coders would help the junior coders learn and advance their skills.

At the end of the current Sprint, you organize a Sprint Retrospective for the coders. It turns out that the group has never conducted a Sprint Retrospective before. You encourage everyone to speak candidly and promise that whatever is said in the Retrospective will not be repeated outside the room.

After a few cautious minutes, the conversation becomes very frank and earnest. The junior coders confess that they feel left out because they cannot keep up with the others. The senior coders feel guilty about not helping the junior coders more, but say they cannot teach the ropes to the beginners and also write the code needed to complete the Increment. The intermediate coders complain about being too busy to do anything more than their own coding work.

When asked how they work with the QA technicians in Ukraine, one of the senior coders describes how the work of a recent Sprint was done. The Sprint began with a Sprint Planning meeting held between the Product Owner in Silicon Valley and the senior coders (who had to stay up late to video chat with the Product Owner during Silicon Valley business hours). The senior coders selected the Product Backlog items to work on and reported the selections to the other coders the next morning. The local team then met and developed a Sprint Backlog that mapped out the tasks necessary to implement the selected Product Backlog items.

After the Sprint Backlog was finished and the work of the Sprint was ready to start, the QA technicians in Ukraine were told which Product Backlog items had been selected. At the end of the Sprint, the completed code was released to the QA team to test. They were expected to use the next Sprint to thoroughly test the code that had been delivered. They were also expected to create tests for the Product Backlog items that had been chosen in the current Sprint so that they could be used for testing during the next Sprint.

Everyone on the coding team was frustrated with how the QA team found and reported defects to be fixed. They used an online tracking tool to report bugs and classify their severity. The worst kind of bug was a "blocker," which meant the testing itself could not proceed until the "block" was removed. The daily bug report often had one or two blockers that had to be fixed immediately. Whichever coder was involved had to drop everything and attend to the problem, then refocus his train of thought so that he could continue the work he had been doing.

The daily bug report disrupted the coders' work even when no blockers were present. An Increment could not be considered "done" if bugs above a certain severity level still existed. The coding team found they had to focus on two objectives at the same time: they had to complete an Increment to give to the QA team at the end of the Sprint, and they had to fix bugs in the prior Increment before it could be considered "done." In practice, the senior and intermediate coders worked on the new Increment and left the debugging work to the junior coders. This is one reason the junior coders felt unimportant and left out.

After spending time with the coders in India, you travel to Kyiv to meet with the QA team. Once again, you find yourself on a large campus with hundreds of technicians working on dozens of projects. The team that was assigned to work for your company consists of just three people, all of them very experienced.

When you organize a Retrospective meeting with the three-person team, you discover that they are considerably frustrated and resentful, too. They say they feel like the tail end of a horse, having to work hard to support the front end but having no say in the direction they are going. They also complain about the front end getting to eat the hay while they must deal with all the "horse sh*t." There is a cynical atmosphere of dark humor among them.

They say it is very difficult to manage their work when they have two objectives all the time: they must test the current Increment carefully and thoroughly, and at the same time, they must analyze the Product Backlog items that the coders have selected and design tests for them for the next Sprint's testing effort. They are always being pressured to report their test results immediately, even if some tests were complicated and difficult to perform. They always must balance the testing of the current Increment with preparing to test the next Increment.

Another source of frustration is that they often have questions about Product Backlog items that require clarification before tests can be designed. It would be better if they could talk with the Product Owner about the items before they are selected for a Sprint. However, they do the best they can when they are given a Product Backlog item to prepare: if they have questions, they often have to send them to the Product Owner via e-mail and wait a day or two for clarification.

Since the QA technicians often get clarifications about Product Backlog items after the coders have started working on them, they frequently design tests for things the coders did not realize were needed. There have been disputes about defects that the coders claimed were not defects at all. The coders have complained about having the requirements changed after their work was "done." The QA testers feel they are caught in the middle.

Bringing the Team Together

After sizing up the situation in Kyiv, you decide to have the QA team visit the coding team in India. You receive permission for the three QA technicians to work alongside the six coders for up to two Sprints before returning to Ukraine.

You begin the meeting with informal introductions, and then arrange a special Retrospective for everyone to raise and discuss various issues. Once again, you encourage everyone to be candid and promise that anything discussed will remain private. After a little while, most of the frustrations each side has had with the other come out. In addition to airing their own frustrations, both sides get to hear the frustrations the other side has had with them. At the end of the meeting, the team has identified a number of areas where they can work together to improve things.

One of the first issues they decide to tackle is a way to make sure everyone understands and agrees on the meaning of each Product Backlog item. Up until now, the coders had analyzed Product Backlog items in order to create the Sprint Backlog task lists needed to implement them. At the same time, the QA technicians also analyzed the Product Backlog items in order to create their tests. The coders would often seek clarifications from the Product Owner about the items while they were writing code. The QA technicians would also seek clarifications from the Product Owner while they were creating their tests. The result was that the coders and the testers often had different interpretations of what the Product Backlog items called for. These differences showed up as bugs in the bug reports and caused arguments about who was "right."

As the Scrum Master, you suggest that they look into ways to use a single analysis of each Product Backlog item to generate both the coding plan and the testing plan. You suggest they look into the various test-first strategies that exist, such as test-driven development (TDD), Acceptance Test Driven Development (ATDD), and Behavior Driven Development (BDD).

In all of these strategies, the QA technicians perform the initial analysis of items. They work with the Product Owner to clarify items by creating tests to check for correct behavior. Once a complete set of tests has been created and reviewed by the Product Owner, the tests can be given to the coders to work from. Since the tests describe the expected behavior of the Increment, they also describe the requirements for the coders to implement.

Because both the coders and the testers work from the same analysis of each Product Backlog item, it is no longer possible for differences in interpretation to exist. The coders and testers both know what is required. Any bugs that are found in testing are true defects and not just different understandings about what is needed.

After a few working sessions, everyone agrees on a plan of action. Before any Product Backlog item can be considered ready to accept into a Sprint, it must be refined by the Product Owner and the QA technicians. Their job is to create a final set of tests that will be used to determine whether a Product Backlog item meets the Definition of Done. When a Product Backlog item is accepted into a Sprint, the coders will create the necessary functionality to pass the tests.

This test-first strategy has a side benefit that turns out to be very valuable. The coders' work can be tested as soon as it is complete, instead of waiting until the next Sprint starts. It becomes possible to deliver a finished Increment in one Sprint instead of two.

Furthermore, a new Sprint routine is now possible. During the first half of a Sprint, the coders are busy writing code for the current Product Backlog items, and the QA technicians spend their time working with the Product Owner to refine future Product Backlog items and develop tests for them. During the second half of the Sprint, the QA technicians turn their attention to running tests on the code the coders have finished, and the coders turn from writing new code to debugging their work. At the end of the Sprint, they will have produced a done and working Increment.

Helping the Junior Coders

The second issue the development team decides to tackle is how to divide the coding work fairly among the senior, intermediate, and junior members of the team. The junior coders want to learn from the senior coders, but the senior coders do not want to take time away from coding in order to teach the beginners.

You suggest that the team consider pair programming, a strategy that is used by many advanced coding teams. In pair programming, two programmers work together to write code. One coder is the "pilot" and the other is the "navigator." As they create solutions for coding problems, they discuss the challenges and various approaches. When they are finished, they have produced a solution that has already been automatically peer reviewed and is usually much cleaner than what would be produced by a single person.

Some people claim it is wasteful to use two programmers to create one program when they could create two programs working alone. This is not true. In practice, two programmers working together can create a much larger amount of clean code in a given period than they can separately. Pair programming is one of the most efficient ways for coders to create finished work. Together, the two programmers can "do it right," rather than having to "do it over."

Another benefit of pair programming is that it lets the programmers learn from each other. It is especially valuable when one member of the pair is very experienced and the other one is less so. Both people benefit, because the junior partner can learn from the senior partner and the senior partner can improve his or her understanding of the craft by explaining things to the junior partner. Explaining something is the most powerful way to solidify one's understanding of it. Pair programming is beneficial for the junior coder, the senior coder, and the coding team as a whole.

After considering the situation, the coders decide to pair up. The two senior coders pair with the two junior coders and the two intermediate coders pair with each other. After a few days, the benefits become obvious and no one considers going back to the old way of doing things.

Conclusion

After two successful Sprints, the QA technicians go back to Ukraine and you go home to Silicon Valley. The teams in India and Ukraine do not lose touch with each other, however.

India and Ukraine are far from Silicon Valley, but they are not too far from each other. The time difference between them is only three and a half hours, so it is possible for the two groups to communicate interactively for several hours each day. They also arrange to send team members to visit each other from time to time to renew their face-to-face relationships.

You have perhaps the hardest time zone challenge. At least once per week, you stay up late to video chat with the development team. Since everyone has worked together face-to-face, the distance is not much of an inconvenience. Talking over the phone with a stranger you have never met is one thing. Talking over the phone with a friend and colleague is another. The friend on the phone may be next door or on the other side of the world. It doesn't matter. Being part of a team is a matter of personal relationships, not proximity.

Case 4:

Company-Standard Story Points

You are a Scrum Master who is just starting with an existing team. You have been hired to "straighten them out." The team is unable to meet their commitments, and the Product Owner must guess when things will be done and those guesses are always incorrect. The team does not have control over themselves or their process.

You ask the Product Owner about the team's velocity—that is, how much Product Backlog the team turns into an Increment during a Sprint. The Product Owner is exasperated. For the past six Sprints, the velocity has ranged from 13 story points to 52 story points. There is no telling what the velocity will be next, as it seems to vary randomly from Sprint to Sprint. "I never know what to say when someone asks me how many Sprints it will take to get to a certain story in the Product Backlog," the Product Owner says. "If the team can't deliver consistent velocity, how can I know what to expect from them?"

You look at the Product Backlog and see that every item has 13 story points. When you ask the Product Owner why that is so, he replies, "That's our company standard. We try to make all stories the same size so that they can be distributed fairly among the developers. It would be unfair to assign someone a 20-point item in a Sprint when someone else gets assigned an eight-point item. Every item has to be 13 points to make sure everyone has an equal burden."

Your assignment:

1. Analyze this situation vis-à-vis the Scrum framework.
2. Create a strategy to deal with the most important problems.

This case illustrates common misconceptions about how story points should be used and how work should be divided among developers on a Scrum Team.

Initial Analysis

When you investigate the Scrum Team's various velocity figures, you notice they are all multiples of 13. Since the Product Owner says that 13 story points is the "company standard," you quickly realize that the velocities recorded over time reflect the number of items that were delivered each Sprint. When the velocity for a Sprint was measured at 13, it means only one item was completed. When the velocity was measured at 52, it means four items were completed. The variations in velocity were easily explained by how many Product Backlog items got finished compared to how many almost made it but were not ready by the end of the Sprint.

Another clue comes from the Product Owner's statement that having all Product Backlog items be of equal size is an attempt to be fair. This implies that each developer on the team is assigned one Product Backlog item at the beginning of each Sprint and is expected to complete it by the end. Some developers are more advanced than others, so it seems that the variations in velocity reflect the fact that the more-experienced developers on the team complete their Product Backlog items most of the time and the less-skilled developers fail to complete their items some of the time.

Applying the Scrum Framework

The Scrum framework gives the development team authority to manage itself in order to create the product improvements identified by the Product Owner. At the beginning of every Sprint, there is a Sprint Planning meeting during which the Product Owner and the development team negotiate the scope of the Sprint's work. The Product Owner identifies valuable improvements to make and the development team chooses the improvements they will undertake based on their understanding of their capacity to get them done.

It is very important for teams to understand what their capacity is. Scrum is based on the principle of empirical process control, which means that important decisions must be based on measured facts as opposed to opinions. For a development team to understand their capacity, they must measure that capacity. They must do some work within a fixed period (such as a Sprint) and then measure how much of that work they actually completed. Once they know how much work they can do, they can make fact-based decisions about how much work they can finish in a Sprint.

Knowing how much work a team can accomplish during a Sprint helps the Product Owner forecast when individual Product Backlog items will be completed and available to customers. If there are 16 Product Backlog items ahead of a particular feature in the Product Backlog and the development team has been able to deliver four completed Product Backlog items per Sprint, some simple arithmetic will allow the Product Owner to forecast that work on the feature in question might start after four more Sprints.

This sounds very simple and straightforward. Unfortunately, it is not. The challenge comes when the development team tries to do the measuring. How does one measure the amount of work that actually got done? It will not do to measure the time that was spent. What we need to know is what was actually accomplished during that time.

It is tempting to gauge the amount of work by estimating the amount of time needed to complete it. However, this makes no sense. It leads to situations where development teams never measure their true capacity. In effect, it turns the question of a team's capacity into "How much time did it take for you to spend a given amount of time?" The question should be "How much time did it take for you to do a given amount of work?"

The fundamental problem is that there is no good unit of measure to use when measuring actual work. It can't be measured in inches or gallons or volts or kilograms. There is no such thing as a work thermometer or a work tape measure. There is no known way to measure the absolute amount of work done in a Sprint.

However, there is a way to get a handle on the size of pieces of work without using absolute measurements. It can be done using relative measurements.

It is possible to say that a task is "big" or "small" without saying exactly how big or how small. If there is one big task and one small task, it is possible to take a third task and decide whether it is bigger than the big task, smaller than the small task, or somewhere in between. If more tasks are added and placed in the range between the bigger and smaller ones, it forms a set of tasks arranged by size. Give the smallest task an arbitrary small value, give the largest task an arbitrary large value, give the remaining tasks values between the smallest one and the largest one, and the result is a usable unit of measure to gauge the relative amount of work the values represent.

In the world of Scrum and Agile, these arbitrary measurements are called story points. Like beauty, their actual "size" is in the eye of the beholder. A large item for one team might be a small item for another team. Story points assigned by one development team cannot be compared to those assigned by another development team. They are only meaningful to the people who go through the exercise of comparing the bigger and smaller tasks.

Story points are critically important for a Scrum Team, though. They are the only known way for a Scrum Team to measure its capacity.

If a team identifies four Product Backlog items as two large items, one medium item, and one small item, and during a Sprint the team members only complete the small item, the medium item, and one of the large items, they can measure their capacity as one large, one medium, and one small item. They should not try to do more than one large, one medium, and one small item if they wish to complete the entire scope they agree to for a Sprint.

As a side note, there is no need to assign numeric values to the story point sizes. Any range of values that increase in size will do. Many Scrum Teams use T-shirt sizes: S, M, L, XL, XXL, and so on.

Refining Product Backlog Items

The Product Owner places items in the Product Backlog that customers will be willing to pay for. Each item represents a problem for the development team to solve or a capability for them to create. The Product Owner sequences them based on his estimate of how valuable they are and how urgently they are needed.

Often, these Product Backlog items are too big for the development team to deliver during a single Sprint. In this situation, the Product Owner and the developers negotiate reductions in the size and scope of the items. They may take one large item and break it into two or more smaller ones. The

Product Owner makes sure the smaller pieces each have measurable value. The developers make sure the smaller pieces are small enough to deliver during a single Sprint. The Product Backlog is then revised, substituting the several smaller pieces for the one overly large one. This negotiation process is called Product Backlog refinement.

Product Backlog refinement is only effective if the sizes of the items are known. Large items cannot be broken into smaller ones if the difference between "large" and "small" is not clear. Story points are used extensively in the Product Backlog refinement process to make it possible for everyone to agree on scaling items for implementation.

Getting the Work Done

The Scrum framework does not assign responsibility for delivering Product Backlog items to individual developers. In Scrum, the development team as a whole negotiates with the Product Owner to accept items to implement in a Sprint. As a result, the development team as a whole is accountable for delivering the items. When the team agrees to a scope, their job is to manage themselves to get the work done. There is no need to be "fair" to individual developers. They divide the work as they see fit and help each other out when necessary. At the end of a Sprint, the development team as a whole either delivers or does not deliver what they forecast. They succeed or fail as a team, together.

There is no assumption within the Scrum framework that a single developer will work on a single Product Backlog item each Sprint. On the contrary, the assumption is that everyone will work on everything as needed and as they see fit. Developers can and should have different skills and different skill levels. They should work on those parts of the task for which they have the best aptitude, energy, and interest. Only they can figure out how to divide the work effectively. The Scrum framework gives them the authority to do so in exchange for accepting responsibility for delivering the items they agree to take on.

What About Fairness?

The organization feels it is very important to treat its developers fairly. In practice, that means it wants to recognize and reward excellent work while sanctioning less-than-excellent results. Top management know full well that excellent developers can perform 10 times better (or more) than their "average" colleagues. Top management want to know who their top performers are and want to make sure they stay happy. They also want to learn who the bottom performers are so that they can be moved out of the organization.

This desire to reward excellent performance is understandable (and even laudable). In practice, though, it runs into some of the same difficulties that occur when trying to measure work. The question then becomes "How can excellence be measured?" What is the unit of measure? What is the yardstick?

It is important to understand that true excellence cannot be measured in terms of effort. It can and should only be measured in terms of results. A developer who works 12-hour days six days per week is not excellent if he or she produces little of value. A developer who works four to five hours per day and takes three- or four-day weekends can be excellent if he or she produces a great deal of value. The only true measure of excellence turns out to be a familiar one: return on investment (ROI). A developer is excellent if he or she produces much more value than it costs to pay him or her to create it.

The value of the work product of a Sprint is easy to measure. All that is required is to get a customer to want it and pay for it. Most of the Product Owner's job revolves around knowing what customers want and will pay for. A competent Product Owner will know the estimated value of each Product Backlog item he or she prioritizes. That knowledge is required, or else the Product Owner cannot make rational decisions about what should be worked on and what should be set aside.

Excellence can be measured by measuring the value of the product compared to the cost of making it. Excellence consists of producing a great deal of value for a small cost. Producing little or no value for a great deal of cost is not excellent at all.

Who Creates Value?

There is one fact that makes it practically impossible to measure the excellence of individual developers. By and large, developers do not create product improvements by themselves. They do their piece of the work and rely on others to do the rest. The amount of value represented by part of a finished product cannot be objectively measured. Only the value of the improvement as a whole can be measured.

Take a typical example: a product improvement involving coding in Java, look-and-feel elements in Cascading Style Sheets (CSS), and database modifications (SQL). Three separate developers are involved in creating the improvement. Did one developer create more value than the other two? If so, which one?

It is impossible to measure which developer added the most value in this situation. The only thing that can be measured is the value of their combined efforts.

Teams create value. Individual developers do not.

Rewarding Excellence

Since excellence is based on results, only the relative excellence of teams can be measured. One team is twice as valuable to a company as another if the first team produces an average of $500,000 of value per Sprint for a cost of $50,000 while the other one produces only $250,000 of value for that same $50,000 cost. A team that produces only $10,000 of value for a $50,000 cost should be dropped.

If the company wants to reward excellence, it must reward the entity that delivered excellent results. In other words, it must reward the entire team when excellence is to be recognized.

Rewarding the team does not mean rewarding all team members equally. The development team jointly accepts responsibility for delivering results. Then the team members manage themselves to distribute the workload and deliver results. If the results are good, the team must jointly accept any reward. Then the team members can manage themselves to divide the reward in a way they deem fair and appropriate.

Scrum Teams manage themselves. This includes selecting the work they do and managing themselves to get it done. This also includes deciding who belongs on the team and who does not. If there is a sluggard in the group, the people who are best able to identify him or her are the other team members the sluggard works with. If a sluggard is hurting the team, the Scrum framework gives the team as a whole the power to "fire" that person. After all, the developers can't be held responsible for delivering results if someone sticks them with a low performer they can't get rid of.

Conclusion

As the Scrum Master, your analysis of the situation leads to the following conclusions.

1. Story points are misunderstood and are being used improperly.
2. The role of teams versus team members is not properly understood.
3. Product Backlog refinement is being used to balance effort rather than preserve value.
4. The development team is using a "one backlog item per developer per Sprint" formula for dividing work rather than creating its own plan for doing so.

As a result of this analysis, the following plan of action is indicated.

1. Educate the Product Owner and the development team about the need to measure the team's capacity to get work done. Explain that there is no absolute way to measure such work. There are only ways to measure the relative sizes of units of work. Encourage the team to adopt a story point-based approach and teach them the proper method for assigning story points to Product Backlog items.
2. Educate the team and the Product Owner about the realities of team-based product development. Emphasize that individual developers cannot create value. Only teams of developers working together can do so. Emphasize that Scrum Teams are given unlimited authority to select the work they do and to manage themselves to do it. They are given this authority in exchange for accepting responsibility for delivering what they agree to deliver.
3. Coach the Product Owner and the development team to undertake effective Product Backlog refinement. The

4. goal of this refinement should not be to create Product Backlog items of equal size. The goal should be to create Product Backlog items no larger than can be implemented during a single Sprint but which still have an objectively measurable value when completed.
5. Teach the development team to create a plan for dividing work once the scope of the upcoming Sprint has been agreed to. They should take the accepted Product Backlog items they selected and create a plan for delivering them. This usually involves breaking the items down into task lists organized around the skills needed to complete the tasks. Such a task list, when coupled with the Product Backlog items they represent, is called the Sprint Backlog in the Scrum framework.

Case 5:

Database Dependencies

You are a Scrum Master and you joined a new company a few weeks ago. After a few days of orientation, you started working with your team. Together, you have just completed the first Sprint Retrospective.

During the Retrospective, one of the developers complained bitterly about a problem she is having with a database administrator (DBA).

The DBAs are located in a central department close to the company's server farm. They spend most of their time tuning the Oracle database cluster so that it performs well. Unfortunately, the company's server farm is located on another continent more than eight time zones away. The time difference makes it hard to communicate with the DBAs in an efficient way.

The DBAs have made a rule that all access to the database must be done with stored procedures. In effect, the database may only be accessed by a kind of program rather than with ad hoc SQL queries. In addition, the DBAs have stated that no stored procedure will be added to the database without the approval of a DBA. This means access to the database is not allowed unless a DBA has approved the specific SQL statements used.

While no one would argue with this kind of restriction being placed on the production database, the DBAs have also restricted access to the near production testing environment. What's more, there is no development sandbox environment for developer use.

The developer in the Retrospective was complaining about the difficulties she has in developing new functionalities requiring database access. If she is to follow the rules, she must design a stored procedure on paper and submit it to the DBAs for approval. Because of the time zone issue, this involves at least a 24-hour turnaround for each request. Often, some question or concern comes back from the DBAs requiring her to revise and resubmit her request, which adds another 24-hour delay.

During the development effort, it is not unusual for her to find that changes are needed for the stored procedure. When the procedure is run in practice, various negative characteristics may become apparent and require correction. The developer then has to submit a request to revise the stored procedure along with a brief justification for doing so.

The developer wants the team to ask for a sandbox version of the Oracle database providing unlimited access for the developers. Her point is that the developers should be free to use ad hoc tools in order to perfect their stored procedures before submitting them to the DBAs. She wants a way to play around with the SQL statements and see the effects of her changes before she submits them to the DBAs to set them in stone.

After the Retrospective is over, you notice two other developers talking quietly with the complaining developer. You overhear them tell her about a clandestine development environment that some of the developers have set up using Amazon Web Services. The clandestine environment is set up using MySQL, so it is not fully compatible with Oracle. Still, the two developers state that it is perfectly adequate for testing their stored procedures prior to submitting them for approval.

Your assignment:

1. Analyze this situation vis-à-vis the Scrum framework.
2. Describe the course of action you would take to deal with this situation.

This case illustrates a typical problem situation involving dependencies between teams with different goals.

Initial Analysis

As you have just joined the company, a little investigation about the origin of the problem is in order. It turns out that the DBAs are being very strict because of earlier challenges with the use of the database.

Up until about a year ago, the developers had unlimited access to both the production and near-production environments. They had command-line-level access and could run ad hoc SQL statements at will. There was no separate DBA group. Any developer who could write SQL statements could make changes to production data.

This led to a failed Sarbanes–Oxley audit. It also led to embarrassing performance problems when large SQL queries were run in the production environment. Worst of all, different development teams would make incompatible changes to the database's structure: one team would break another team's functionality, and when the other team fixed the "bug," they would break the first team's work.

This chaotic situation led to the creation of a separate DBA group whose goal was to protect the integrity and performance of the database. Command-line access for running ad hoc SQL statements was restricted to the DBA group. Every SQL statement had to be evaluated for its effect on database integrity and performance before it could be run. The DBAs instituted the stored procedure rule because stored procedures allow the DBAs to see and evaluate the exact SQL statements proposed by the developers. They would only add the stored procedures to the database if they felt they were safe and effective.

The Scrum Team developers in the company understood and accepted the need to protect the production database. What they questioned was the reason for stringent protection of the near-production testing database. The DBA group's answer was that it makes no sense to allow unverified SQL statements to be run in the test environment if they could not be run in the production environment. Testing with anything other than stored procedures proved nothing, as only stored procedures could be moved to production.

The DBAs pointed to the fact that evaluating stored procedures helped them catch potentially serious mistakes in the SQL statements prior to being run. Poorly constructed SQL queries can greatly affect performance, and poorly thought out structural changes can greatly impact data integrity. The DBAs' stored procedure rule unquestionably stopped several serious situations from happening. The chaos that led to the creation of the DBA group has been eradicated for all intents and purposes.

The developers acknowledge the improvement in database integrity and performance. At the same time, though, they point to the fact that the delivery of new functionality has slowed to a crawl. They estimate that they are only about 30% as productive as they were before the DBAs locked things down. The time zone differences and the 24-hour cycle time for questions and responses are causing their own impacts. The Product Owner is concerned that not enough value is being delivered to justify the expense of continuing to develop the product.

Applying the Scrum Framework

The Scrum framework calls for products to be developed by self-managing, cross-functional teams. A self-managing team is one that accepts responsibility for creating a product and manages itself to do so. A cross-functional team is one that has all the skills and capabilities within it to create a product. A team must have the ability to create a product if it is going to accept responsibility for doing so. If it does not hold all the cards, it cannot play the game and win. If it does not have the talents, resources, and permissions to take a Product Owner's idea and turn it into something in the hands of a customer, it cannot be held accountable for not doing so. In situations where capabilities are divided, usually no one is accountable for delivering results.

In this case study, several teams are working on different aspects of one product. Some of the problems that led to the creation of the DBA group were the result of the teams interfering with each other.

When several teams are working to create a single product, which team is accountable for the results? According to the Scrum framework (and its scaled Scrum variants), all of them are. The teams must manage themselves to solve problems and deliver value. When there are issues of dependency and/or interference, they must manage themselves and their work so as to deal with them.

The DBA group was created to deal with and fix some serious problems. Unfortunately, creating the group was the wrong way to address those problems. Giving the responsibility of protecting the database to the DBAs took it away from the rest of the developers. They were no longer on the hook to prevent the problems they had caused. Their productivity suffered, but they could deflect blame by pointing fingers at the "overly strict" DBA group.

The DevOps Model

Many software products provide value by offering services through an online portal of some sort. These portals must be supported by technicians who deal with servers, networks, and other components necessary to run the portals. One of these components is usually a database engine of some kind. Traditionally, these component technicians are called the operations group. They provide support needed to operate the software created by the development group. Again, traditionally speaking, the DBA group falls under the operations umbrella.

Scrum Teams must be cross-functional, which means they must be able to own the creation and delivery of the product they develop. Their responsibility is to take a need identified by the Product Owner and put a solution for it into the hands of a customer. Writing software is part of their responsibility, but with products like portals, the duty really should not end there. To put a portal-based solution into a customer's hands, the developers also need to deal with the servers, networks, database engines, and other components traditionally called "operations." They must be accountable for creating the whole solution, not just the software portion of it.

This need led to the development of the DevOps model for managing development teams. The term *DevOps* comes from combining *Development* and *Operations*. The idea is to put software creators and service delivery technicians on the same team so that they can work closely together. The service delivery technicians help the software creators avoid creating functions that are difficult to run in production. The software creators can get help from the service delivery technicians for exploring the capabilities of the hardware used. Together, they can accept accountability for delivering value. In exchange, they can be given authority to manage themselves and make their own decisions.

Scaling the Solution

Implementing the DevOps model will address only part of the problem that gave rise to the DBA group. An additional strategy is needed to address the rest of the problem. The DBAs were formed in part because different teams working on the product were interfering with each other. One team made structural database changes that fouled things up for the other team, and vice versa. The DevOps model will not prevent this kind of trouble. Another solution is needed.

The challenge is to keep different Scrum development teams from interfering with each other. Interference occurs when actions are taken without realizing they will affect others. These effects are called dependencies. Whenever two or more teams are working on a single product, these dependencies must be managed and controlled. The key to managing and controlling dependencies is to make them known to everyone involved. The key is to make dependencies transparent.

The various scaled Scrum models differ in many ways, but one thing they have in common is a mechanism for making dependencies transparent. Trouble happens when one team takes an action that affects another team without realizing it. Making dependencies transparent eliminates the possibility of affecting someone else without realizing it. The conflicting need may still be there, but at least everyone affected can see it and work it out together. The goal is “no surprises.”

An example of a mechanism for making dependencies transparent comes from the Nexus Exoskeleton for the Scrum framework. In Nexus, the Product Backlog refinement activity includes a requirement for identifying potential dependencies. These dependencies are tracked during a Sprint and made transparent by the Nexus Integration Team and the Nexus Sprint Backlog. The status of the dependencies is reviewed in the Nexus Daily Scrum.

The Nexus Integration Team is accountable for the creation of an integrated Increment at the end of each Sprint with all related dependencies resolved.

Developing a Coaching Strategy

After a full analysis of the situation, it is apparent that a good solution would be to use a scaled Scrum framework to manage dependencies and development teams along the DevOps model. This model will give development teams the full set of skills they need to be able to deliver the product. The scaled Scrum framework will let them manage their joint efforts effectively.

You hold a Big Room meeting with all the technical people involved: the software writers, DBAs, and operational support technicians. Since they are not all in the same physical location, the meeting is held virtually using an appropriate online conferencing tool.

The purpose of the meeting is to introduce the DevOps model and the scaled Scrum framework you have chosen to use. After these ideas are introduced, you ask the group to supply a small team of people to refine the Product Backlog with the Product Owner. The purpose of this refinement exercise is to identify potential dependencies to be resolved.

Sometime later, after the dependencies in the Product Backlog have been identified, you hold another Big Room meeting. This meeting is the Sprint Planning meeting for the upcoming Sprint. You ask the full development team to group dependent Product Backlog items together as much as possible; in other words, group the ones that will affect the database structure together, group the ones that will affect the user interface look and feel together, and so on. After the items have been grouped, you ask the developers to form teams to tackle sets of items. One team will deal with the database issues, another one will handle the user interface issues, and other teams will be responsible for the other dependency-related items. If some groups of dependent items are too large for one team to handle, they can form more than one team with the caveat that those teams must work closely together.

After the teams have been formed around the related items, you dismiss the Big Room meeting and ask the groups to get together individually and make their work plans for the Sprint. When the Sprint Backlogs are created, the groups start working. You ask them to send representatives to a combined Daily Scrum meeting to make transparent any issues that might impede the successful creation of an integrated Increment by the end of the Sprint.

Since the DBAs are now part of the team (or teams) implementing database changes, they can now make sure any SQL statements are problem free as they are being formulated, rather than trying to do so after the fact. Since any structural changes are being made by a small, known set of teams, the DBAs on those teams can work together to make those changes safe and effective.

It might even be possible for the Product Backlog items involving database changes to be worked on by just a single team. In that case, there are no dependencies to worry about.

At the end of the Sprint, you convene another Big Room meeting to review the functionality of the new version of the product produced by the Sprint. You ask the Product Owner to invite anyone she wishes to the review, and encourage her to discuss what she expected to see and her reactions to the new version of the product. You also ask her to talk about new ideas to put into the Product Backlog.

At the end of the review, you ask everyone in the Big Room meeting to talk about any lessons learned during the Sprint. After the meeting is finished, you encourage the individual teams to get together and discuss their own lessons learned.

The next morning, you call another Nexus Sprint Planning meeting and start the process over again.

Conclusion

The fundamental problem posed in this case study is a lack of cross-functionality. The developers did not have the ability to create the product without the cooperation of the DBA group. The goal of the DBA group was to prevent damage to the database, whereas the goal of the developers was to change and enhance it. They were working at cross-purposes.

The problems that led to the DBA group being formed in the first place were caused by failing to properly manage dependencies between teams. The DBAs were acting to protect the database from damage caused by conflicting changes made by different development teams.

The solution to the problem lay in creating truly cross-functional teams using the DevOps model. In addition, a scaled Scrum framework was used to identify and manage dependencies so that they could not cause trouble.

Case 6:

Expanding Offshore

You are a Scrum Master. You have joined a medium-size company with a small IT department and a big project to complete.

The IT staffers maintain and enhance a legacy enterprise resource planning (ERP) application running on big iron and used for the company's product distribution business. The company publishes a catalog of products that it distributes, and employs call center staffers who take phone orders and key them into the ERP application. Then the orders are processed and sent to 21 warehouses throughout North America for fulfillment.

The company's chief operating officer (COO) has decided to sponsor a project to create an e-commerce website. Instead of relying on phone orders, the COO wants to let customers search an online version of the catalog and place items into a shopping cart. At checkout, the shopping cart contents should be fed directly into the ERP system for fulfillment.

It is clear that the existing IT staff have no expertise in web development. Budgetary constraints also dictate that any new staff must be sourced from offshore to keep costs down.

Your assignment:

1. Analyze the situation vis-à-vis the Scrum framework.
2. Come up with a strategy to utilize an onshore–offshore model to create the website.

This case illustrates some of the challenges of trying to add new technologies to an existing platform.

Initial Analysis

The Scrum framework calls for products to be created by self-managing, cross-functional teams. A cross-functional team possesses all the skills necessary to create the product without any outside help. A self-managing team manages itself and accepts responsibility for delivering a valuable product. In exchange, it has full authority to decide how the product will be made.

The COO's decision to develop the website poses a problem of cross-functionality. The existing team is proficient at programming for a legacy system but has no skills or experience creating websites. The team has to augment its skill set in order to deliver this new functionality. As stated in the case description, these new skills need to come from an offshore company because of budgetary constraints.

Another concern is how to use the Scrum framework properly to organize the website development effort. Scrum defines various roles, responsibilities, events, and artifacts. How should the Scrum roles be divided? What form should the artifacts take? How about the Scrum events: what form should they take?

Identifying the Product

The first step is to identify the product. The Scrum framework is organized around products owned by Product Owners. Scrum development teams work to create product features identified and prioritized by Product Owners.

A product is something that can be produced and has an objectively measurable value. If the value cannot be measured, there is no way to know whether the development effort is worthwhile or not.

What is the product in this case? Until this new initiative was launched, the product was the legacy platform. Its value could be measured by calculating the revenue represented by the orders it processed, and its efficiency could be measured by calculating the cost of processing and fulfilling an order with it. Valuable improvements would be ones that would either increase the number of orders processed or reduce the cost per order of processing them.

Now that the COO has proposed this new website, the question becomes whether the new website is a product in and of itself, or whether it is simply an improvement to the existing platform. If it is a stand-alone product, it should have its own Product Owner and Product Backlog.

The COO sees the value of the website in terms of both increasing order revenue and decreasing order processing costs. A website can accept orders 24 hours per day, seven days per week, whereas the call center staff only work during business hours. Allowing customers to place orders 24-7 should make it more convenient for them to place orders. This should lead them to choose to buy from this company rather than from its less-convenient competitors.

It is relatively expensive to take orders using call center staff. If an order taker is paid $100 per day and takes in 25 orders, each order costs $4 to receive. Having customers key orders directly into the system adds no additional cost.

It is clear, then, that the way to measure the value of the website is to measure its effect on the value of the legacy platform. A more accurate way to name and identify the actual product is to recognize that the product is the order entry process and not the legacy platform. The latter is an old solution to the order entry problem, and the website is an improvement to that old solution. Therefore, the new website is not a stand-alone product. It should share a Product Owner and Product Backlog with the legacy platform.

Who should the Product Owner be? The answer is obvious. The COO should be the Product Owner. He owns the order entry process and is responsible for maximizing the value it produces.

Solving the Problem of Cross-Functionality

A Scrum development team cannot accept responsibility for creating a product it doesn't have the capability to make. It must find a way to add to its skills in order to fulfill its obligations. In this case, there is an additional constraint: the team must add the necessary skills without causing the company to spend more money than it can afford to spend.

A few Internet searches turn up many website development resources in low-cost parts of the world. They offer many choices in terms of the look and feel they could create. The question is how to find and choose the right resource to fill the need.

The choice of resources is a technical one and must be made by the development team. But first they must refine the need in order to understand it. They conduct a refinement exercise and conclude that the resource must be able to create the following:

- A website with convenient features and a good look and feel
- A custom shopping cart that can feed orders into the legacy system using a custom interface created by the local development team
- The resource must be able to create ways for the website to send price and availability inquiries to the legacy system and display the responses to the customer

- A way for the website to gather customer credentials and validate them against customer profile information stored in the legacy system

Boiling this down further, the development team concludes that they need a resource that can create the following:

- An attractive website
- The functionality necessary to exchange information with legacy system interfaces created by the original programmers

Using this information, they narrow down the search and identify a few offshore companies as finalists. After further discussions and negotiations, they settle on a company in Asia.

They negotiate a deal whereby the partner company in Asia is compensated on a "flat rate per Sprint" basis. At the beginning of each Sprint, a Sprint Planning meeting is used to agree on the scope of work to be accomplished. At the end of each Sprint, a Sprint Review is conducted. If the accomplishments are satisfactory, the partner's fee is paid and the next Sprint is initiated. If the accomplishments are not satisfactory, the fee is held until any discrepancies are resolved.

Addressing Time Zone and Language Differences

Adding the partner company did not turn all the developers into a single team that could manage itself easily. If the website developers ran into a website-related problem, the legacy programmers could not help them with it. Nor could the website developers help the legacy programmers. One group understood COBOL and the other understood Java. Even worse, one group understood English and the other mostly understood Chinese.

Further complicating the communication problems was the fact that the end of the workday for the local programmers was the beginning of the workday for the partner company. There was only a short window of time each day when both teams of technical people were awake and at work. This made spur-of-the-moment communication between the different teams almost impossible. Information was exchanged via e-mail (with the inevitable time lag for the response) or it was made part of formal meetings scheduled well in advance.

All of these challenges meant the website and the legacy staff had to work as independently as possible. Extensive dependencies between them would strangle any progress. The work had to be organized in such a way that the need for communication between the teams was as close to zero as possible. In effect, they had to function as two separate teams working on the same product.

Applying a Scaled Scrum Framework

Using the Scrum framework with multiple teams is called scaled Scrum. There are several different variants of the scaled Scrum idea, but they all agree on the overall approach: there is one product, one Product Owner, and a group of developers who organize themselves into several individual teams to create the product together.

The Product Owner does not care whether one team or many teams create the product. The Product Owner's job remains the same: he or she must create a Produ t Backlog of problems to solve or capabilities to create; identify the value of implementing each Product Backlog item; and prioritize these items in such a way that the developers can create the most value when they work through the list.

In scaled Scrum, the Product Backlog refinement process takes on additional importance. The Product Backlog items must be adjusted so that they are not too big to accomplish in a Sprint and so that single teams can accomplish them with as few dependencies as possible. When dependencies are unavoidable, they must be made transparent so that they can be resolved without impacting other work (if possible).

In scaled Scrum, there is a single Sprint Planning meeting during which the Sprint scope is agreed to, and there is a single Sprint Review during which the combined work of all the teams is reviewed. Other than those two occasions, the various development teams are free to work independently. Their only coordination obligation is to make the status of any dependencies transparent to the other development teams.

Refining the Product Backlog

The COO (as Product Owner) creates a high-level Product Backlog of items for the website using the user story format. A user story is a statement of need and the reason for that need from the point of view of an identifiable user of the product. For instance, “As a customer, I wish to check the price and availability of an item so that I can decide whether to buy it or not” is a requirement in proper user story form. The identifiable user is “a customer,” the need is “check the price and availability of an item,” and the reason for the need is to “decide whether to buy it or not.”

When refining such a user story, it quickly becomes apparent that three separate technical challenges are involved. There is a look-and-feel challenge of capturing the inquiry information and displaying the results; a legacy platform challenge of assembling the information to satisfy the inquiry; and a challenge in creating an interface to receive the inquiry from the website and return the response from the legacy platform.

Almost all the Product Backlog items involve these three challenges in one way or another. They all require website design work, legacy platform back-end processing, and an interface mechanism for exchanging inquiries and responses.

The technical people quickly realize that figuring out the interface mechanism is the most urgent technical challenge to be addressed. Once the interface mechanism is defined, the rest of the problem will only consist of defining which pieces of information need to be exchanged. Using the above example, if the technical people figure out how to exchange the information necessary for a price and availability inquiry, they will know how to exchange information for any inquiry or process.

After conferring with one another, the legacy developers and the website developer agree to exchange information using XML documents posted via HTTP. Once this basic mechanism is created, all the necessary cross-platform interactions can be implemented simply by defining a different XML document for each one.

Working Together Independently

The Product Backlog refinement process is conducted via video chats during the brief window of time every day when normal business hours in the United States and Asia coincide. Items are refined into descriptions of specific actions, such as the previously mentioned price and availability inquiry function. A refined Product Backlog item has a description of the user interface look and feel, a description of the processing required on the legacy platform, and a list of data elements to be exchanged via the XML/HTTP mechanism.

At the start of each Sprint, a Sprint Planning meeting is held via video chat, once again during the brief period when it is late afternoon in the United States and morning in the partner's location in Asia. During the meeting, the developers select a number of Product Backlog items to implement during the Sprint. For each item they accept, they double-check the list of data elements to be exchanged.

When the list of Product Backlog items for the Sprint is finalized and agreed to, the video chat ends. The legacy platform people then create a Sprint Backlog reflecting the work they have to do to consume and reply to the agreed-upon XML data elements. The website developers also create a Sprint Backlog reflecting the work they have to do to generate inquires and consume responses according to the agreed-upon XML data elements.

As long as the content and structure of the agreed-upon XML transactions do not change, the two development teams can work independently of each other. There are no real dependencies that could impede either team's progress. During the early stages of the Sprint, both teams test their work by simulating the responses of the other side. Toward the end, they test their work by connecting their functions through the actual interface.

Both teams conduct a Daily Scrum meeting, but they do so separately. After all, there is no need to confer. The developers in Asia use their Daily Scrum to deal with website-related challenges and the legacy developers use theirs to focus on legacy platform issues. They only need to talk if an issue arises that calls for changing the XML data elements to be exchanged. They exchange brief status e-mails reporting progress, but nothing more is needed.

At the end of each Sprint, a Sprint Review meeting is conducted. Once again, it occurs via video chat at the appropriate time of day. The functionality of the website and the legacy system is demonstrated and discussed. The Product Owner uses the review to refine his vision of the final product, and new Product Backlog items are often added.

After the Sprint Review, each team conducts a Sprint Retrospective. If any conclusions are reached that involve the other team, they are shared via e-mail. If necessary, a joint Sprint Retrospective meeting is scheduled and held via video chat to discuss any significant issues involving both teams.

Measuring Delivered Value

In this case study, the website went live with a few key functions after development had been underway for approximately three months. It proved to be popular. Within six months, it accounted for 30% of the company's daily order revenue. About two-thirds of this volume came from customers who had placed telephone orders in the past. About one-third came from entirely new customers.

The Product Owner soon realizes that money can be saved by moving other customer interactions to the website and away from phone calls. Some of the later additions to the Product Backlog are order status inquiries, outstanding invoice inquiries, credit card payment processing, and a shipping calculator. All of these are justified based on reducing the cost of these common customer interactions. The actual cost reductions are readily measurable based on the reduced need for telephone support staff.

The actual out-of-pocket cost of creating the website functionality ends up being about 5% to 10% of the cost of similar websites created with U.S.-based resources. The increase in orders plus the processing cost reductions mean the website investment is paid back in a matter of months. The ROI of the website is calculated at more than 175%.

Conclusion

The Scrum framework can be used very successfully in onshore–offshore contexts. Whenever teams must work in separate locations, the key to success is to eliminate dependencies. This can be done by carefully structuring the work so that teams and their work products interact through agreed-upon interfaces. In effect, teams must be loosely bound rather than tightly bound. The members of a team must interact constantly to achieve their goals. Members of different teams must interact as little as possible so as to avoid disrupting one another's work.

While the different teams in a scaled Scrum context must work as independently as possible, they should all remain focused on the goal of delivering value. In this case, both the website work and the legacy platform processing were necessary to create a working solution. Neither the website nor the back-end processing that made it work had any value on its own. Only the combination offered something that customers wanted.

The Scrum developers found a way to solve the problem of cross-functionality they faced. By doing so, they were able to accept responsibility for creating the improvements the company needed.

Case 7:

The Java Nazi

You are a developer with Professional Scrum Developer certification. You are a strong Java programmer and you have been assigned to a Scrum development team that is having trouble. You are being asked to get the team back on track. The Scrum Team has no Scrum Master, as the company does not believe such people are necessary.

It does not take long to identify one of the major issues. There is a developer on the team who is very hard to deal with. The others have given her the nickname “Java Nazi,” and she insists on reviewing and criticizing everyone else’s work.

During the Sprint Planning meeting, she selects the Product Backlog items that will be done and assigns them to the other developers. During the Daily Scrums, she insists on having everyone report their status to her. Then she updates the Scrum board in Ralley, the team’s online project management tool, and lets the Product Owner know the board is up-to-date. During the Sprint Review, she demonstrates the team’s work and answers the Product Owner’s questions. During the Sprint Retrospective, she asks the other team members to report to her what they have done to improve things during the Sprint.

The team has not delivered much value for quite a while. The Java Nazi keeps selecting more and more Product Backlog items for the team each Sprint, but fewer and fewer of them seem to get done. Lately she has been complaining privately to the Product Owner that the others on the team are “no good.” She is asking the Product Owner to fire everyone and let her put together a new team.

One of the reasons you were hired is to see whether the Java Nazi is right or not. The Product Owner hired you without the Java Nazi's input. The Product Owner wants to know whether the other developers are strong enough in their skills to get the job done.

Your assignment:

1. Analyze this situation vis-à-vis the Scrum framework.
2. Come up with a strategy to deal with this and outline the first few steps.

This case illustrates a common challenge involving development team self-management.

Initial Analysis

Scrum development teams are given the authority to manage themselves as they see fit. They organize the work they do without outside influences. No one outside the team can force them to take any steps they do not choose to take themselves.

At the same time, the development team is accountable for delivering value. They are given authority over the scope and manner of their work in exchange for accepting accountability for producing more value than it costs to employ them.

The fundamental problem to be addressed here is not that the Java Nazi is dominating things. If the development team chooses to be dominated and the Java Nazi chooses to do it, that is entirely up to them. The Scrum framework principle of self-management gives them the right to do so.

The fundamental problem here is that the development team is not producing much value. In fact, it is producing less and less value as time goes on. The development team can indeed be held accountable for failing to deliver value. A Scrum framework Product Owner is an investor, after all. If he or she concludes that the development team is a bad investment, it is the Product Owner's responsibility to pull the plug and invest the money elsewhere. The members of a development team that produces little value may soon end up unemployed.

The members of this development team keep themselves very busy. They get their assignments from the Java Nazi and spend each Sprint working on them. By the time the Sprint is over, a number of new product "pieces" are ready to go. Unfortunately, they rarely fit together properly. More likely than not, a key part of the product did not get completed or does not work as expected. Only about 30% of the Product Backlog items selected for a given Sprint end up with solutions that meet the Definition of Done. The rest go back on the Product Backlog for future consideration and/or rework.

A Scrum framework development team manages itself to deliver value. If little value is delivered, it means the team is not managing itself very effectively.

How Did This Situation Develop?

You decide to have a number of one-on-one talks with the development team members. Your goal is to evaluate their individual skills (as requested by the Product Owner) as well as determine whether the team is cross-functional enough to create the product. You also want to find out how the relationship between the Java Nazi and the other team members developed into what it is now.

The development team consists of people with an average level of skill and experience in most areas. The database person is fairly experienced, the UX/UI people can produce attractive and functional designs, and the testing/QA people do their work effectively.

The one area where the team is not very strong is in Java coding. The Java Nazi is the only one with significant experience in this area. The others are all at the beginner or junior level. They rarely try to disagree with what the Java Nazi says.

You also note that the team has difficulty delivering Product Backlog items involving significant Java coding. Most of the Product Backlog items not involving major Java work are delivered as forecast, but most of the items with significant new Java functionality are not finished by the end of each Sprint.

The Scrum framework makes clear that a Scrum Team is responsible for managing itself. This responsibility includes selecting its own members. The membership of the team is up to the team itself. They should make sure they have the necessary skills to be cross-functional and to make the product without outside help. They also must make sure they have the necessary level of skills to get the job done.

It turns out that the membership of this team has changed since the Java Nazi joined. When she first arrived there were two other experienced Java developers working on the team. The team hired the Java Nazi to help these developers catch up, as Java coding had proved to be a bottleneck.

These two developers welcomed the Java Nazi because of her skills and experience, but it didn't take long before conflicts developed. Within a few Sprints, all three of them were arguing constantly. The two original developers ended up leaving. When the team searched for replacements for them, the Java Nazi insisted on having the final say. She turned down experienced candidates and accepted junior coders who would do what she told them to do.

When it comes time for you to have a one-on-one talk with the Java Nazi, she cancels several appointments at the last minute because of "emergencies." She finally says she can afford to spend 10 minutes with you before she goes home on the upcoming Friday evening. When the time comes, she is very guarded and suspicious. She gives empty answers to every question and accuses you of working with the Product Owner to try to take her job away.

Who Is to Blame?

As a Professional Scrum Developer, you know all the members of a Scrum development team are accountable for the team's results. Since it requires a number of divergent skills to create modern software solutions, the contributions of individual team members cannot be singled out as "especially valuable." Only the combined work product of all the team members can have value. Since only the team as a whole is capable of creating value, the team as a whole is accountable for doing so.

It is clear that the Java Nazi has acquired quite a bit of control over the team. She chooses its workload, assigns tasks, and reports results. She selects its members and ensures that no one will join the team who can challenge her authority.

She is very suspicious of you because you joined the team without her consent. The Product Owner did not even give her the chance to check you out. She sees you as a threat, and you expect her to do everything she can to discredit you in the eyes of the Product Owner.

So, is the Java Nazi the problem? Put another way, will getting rid of the Java Nazi solve all the problems?

The answer is no.

Where Does Power Come From?

During the one-on-one conversations, many developers asked you to take control. They noted that your own Java skills are at the expert level and you have a great deal of experience. They want you to challenge the Java Nazi and make her give up control. They want you to take over. They want you to run the team instead of her.

You have many years of experience working in many different organizations. Those years have taught you quite a bit about the nature of power. The Java Nazi is exercising a great deal of power, but you are experienced enough to know where the Java Nazi's power is coming from.

You know people like the Java Nazi talk about taking power. You also know power can never be taken.

The Java Nazi has power over the team because the team has given her that power. They don't need you to take it away from her. They need to take back the power they have given her.

Accepting Responsibility

The Java Nazi has no special or formal authority over the team. She simply acts as though she does. She has strong opinions and stronger preferences. She is not afraid to state them. She even dares people to disagree with her. She gets her way again and again because no one dares to stand up to her.

One reason the various team members give her the power to control them is that it helps them avoid responsibility. She provides a ready-made excuse for failure. If she assigns work to a developer, the developer does not have to take any responsibility for the results.

If the Java Nazi assigns work a developer can do and the developer completes it successfully, all is well. If the developer cannot complete the work successfully, it is not necessarily the developer's fault. The Java Nazi may have assigned something too big or too complicated for the developer to do. The Java Nazi is to blame here, as she should have known the task was too difficult before assigning it to the developer.

If the work the Java Nazi assigns turns out to be the wrong thing to do to add value to the product, once again it is not the developer's fault. The developer just did as he or she was told. If it turned out not to be valuable, it is the Java Nazi's fault for assigning a worthless task for the developer to do.

The development team does not like the Java Nazi's abrasiveness, but they do like being able to hide behind her decisions. They would be happy if you were to take over the Java Nazi's role. They see you as kind and helpful whereas the Java Nazi is mean and selfish. They want a kind and helpful person to manage them. They want you to manage them nicely, but they still want someone to relieve them of the burden of responsibility. They want to be told what to do. They would prefer to be told by someone who is nice about it.

The only way to fix this situation is to get the team to accept the responsibility they are avoiding. They must be made to realize that their future is in their own hands. If the team does not start producing more value soon, no excuses will help them. No one will care that it was the Java Nazi who made the bad choices for them. The lack of value produced will be reason enough to get rid of everyone.

Using the Sprint Retrospective Properly

The Scrum framework contains an event specifically intended to help teams improve the way they manage themselves. At the end of every Sprint, the Product Owner, the Scrum Master, and the development team get together to discuss ways to improve how the team works together. This meeting is called the Sprint Retrospective.

The Retrospective depends on transparency. It must be a frank discussion about real issues. Its purpose is to bring out all the elephants in the room that everyone knows are there but no one is brave enough to acknowledge. It is a problem-solving exercise, and it depends on being able to talk about problems without fear of repercussions.

To make it safe to talk about issues, the Sprint Retrospective must be a closed meeting. No one can attend other than the people involved: the Product Owner, the Scrum Master (if any), and the development team. No record is kept of the discussion unless everyone present agrees to it. No report of the discussion is made to anyone outside the group, nor is any needed. The discussions and any conclusions only affect the full Scrum Team and are no one else's business.

Up until now, the Sprint Retrospectives held by the team have not been the problem-solving sessions they should have been. You decide that the next Sprint Retrospective must be different.

You have a talk with the Product Owner and explain the correct function of the Sprint Retrospective. You ask the Product Owner to attend and to be ready to be very transparent about the lack of value delivered. You ask him to be very clear about what that means for the future of the team. You warn him that the Retrospective meeting may be a long one.

Addressing the Elephant in the Room

When the Sprint Review for the current Sprint comes to an end, the team reconvenes in a conference room with a table, chairs, and a whiteboard. The Java Nazi starts to ask for developer reports as usual, but you interrupt and bring the Product Owner into the room. You explain that this time, the Sprint Retrospective will be conducted differently. It will be a closed meeting so that everyone can speak freely. Its purpose is to have an open discussion about challenges facing the team. No record will be kept of what is said, but if the team wishes to publish any conclusions when the meeting is finished, they may do so as long as everyone agrees.

Then you ask the Product Owner to talk about the lack of value delivered by the team over the past few months. He points out that the team's salaries plus the cost of office space, equipment, and other charges is a very large sum of money. Over the past few months, these costs have been more than two times higher than the value of the Increments that were delivered. If the situation doesn't improve, the product will be phased out and the team will be laid off.

At this point, you shift the discussion. You turn to the developers and say, "So, now you know where we stand. There is no way to get around it. We have to find a way to deliver more value. If we don't, we won't be here very long."

What follows is a long, emotional discussion about many problems that have been pushed into the background and ignored. There are several heated exchanges between the Java Nazi and the others. You point out that the team is in this together and must figure out the solutions. You note that the Product Owner's future is on the line as well: if the product is phased out, what will the Product Owner be needed for?

During the discussion, you go to the whiteboard and start writing things down. You ask for specific things the team can do differently to solve specific problems. You make a list of the problems on the left side of the board and a list of actions to address those problems on the right side of the board. You ask the team to rate the problems as “extremely serious,” “very serious,” “serious,” or “not very serious,” and you ask them to rate the actions to address the problems as “extremely difficult,” “very difficult,” “difficult,” or “not very difficult.”

You note that during the discussion, the Java Nazi has a number of strong opinions and attempts to force her ideas onto the team. You deal with that by adding her opinions to the whiteboard lists and asking the team for their ratings of them.

After everyone agrees that the lists are complete, you ask the team to review them and to choose some actions to take. You stress that the team must only choose the actions they feel they can accomplish by the end of the next Sprint. For each action, they must identify the problem they wish to address and specify a way to measure the effect the action had on the targeted problem.

The Sprint Retrospective does not adjourn until everyone is satisfied with the action plan that was produced. This includes both the development team and the Product Owner. The action plan is added to the to-do list for the next Sprint. The items on the action plan become Sprint Backlog items. They join the other items that are required in order to deliver the Product Backlog items that the Product Owner and the development team agree to in the upcoming Sprint Planning meeting.

After the next Sprint is over, a Sprint Retrospective is held during which the team discusses the results of the actions that were taken, makes a new list of problems and solutions, and selects the next steps to take.

Conclusion

After this initial Sprint Retrospective, the team came up with the following actions.

1. All Product Backlog items will be refined by the entire development team and not just by the Java Nazi.
2. During the Sprint Planning meeting, no Product Backlog item will be accepted into a Sprint unless the development team accepts it unanimously.
3. The entire team is responsible for delivering every item it accepts. If one developer runs into trouble with an item, everyone else must step in to make sure the work gets done.
4. The Product Owner must assign a realistic value to each Product Backlog item so that the team knows how much value it is delivering each Sprint.
5. The development team will evaluate the skills of its members and decide whether they have the correct mix of skills to deliver the product.

The question remains, however, as to what to do with the Java Nazi. Should she be included in the team going forward, or should she be let go?

According to the Scrum framework, the development team has control over its own membership. If the entire team wants the Java Nazi to leave the team, they have the power to ask her to go.

At the same time, the Java Nazi caused trouble because the rest of the team allowed her to do so. There was a leadership vacuum and she stepped in to fill it. The others let her do this because she provided an excuse for failure: they did not need to blame themselves if they could just blame her.

Once the team stepped up and shouldered its responsibilities, the Java Nazi could no longer dominate them. She could express her opinions but could not enforce them without the consent of the others. She stayed on and contributed her considerable Java skills to the general success of the team.

In the end, a Scrum Team manages itself. Whether the Java Nazi stayed or went was just one decision among many made under the principle of self-management.

Case 8:

Organizing 75 New Developers

You are a Scrum Master who has just been hired by The a large Silicon Valley technology company. The company practically created an entire industry in the 1990s and has dominated its niche for many years. Lately it has attracted numerous competitors that have introduced several innovative products much faster that the company has. The company wants to regain its former leadership position in the industry.

To do so, the company has launched an initiative to create a state-of-the-art tool using newly developed software technology. The company wants to set the standard for how its new technology is used, just as it set the standard in the 1990s for products using its old technology. At that time, the company's competitors had to develop products that were compatible with its technology. The company wants to own this new niche so that its competitors will again have to develop products that are compatible with its technology.

A relatively young and aggressive executive who is a rising star within the company is spearheading the initiative. The executive sought and received approval from the board of directors to hire 75 junior-level engineers to develop the product at an accelerated pace. The human resources department has recruited 75 recent graduates of Ivy League colleges and universities and is currently onboarding them.

The executive pushing the initiative tells you he expects the first version of the new product to be in customers' hands within six months. He says the timing is critical, because others are trying to capitalize on this new technology as well. The first company to field a product using this new technology will have a tremendous market advantage. He says the future of the company hangs on the success of this initiative.

You have been hired to organize the 75 engineers into Scrum Teams that will work together effectively. Organizing 75 new hires at the same time is a tall order. You will need to figure out how to tackle the challenge.

Your assignment:

1. Analyze this situation vis-à-vis the Scrum framework.
2. Come up with a strategy to deal with this.

This case illustrates a common set of mistakes often made when gearing up a new product development effort.

Initial Analysis

After some investigation, you realize the executive has made several serious mistakes in launching this initiative.

First, he wants to create a product that will dominate a new industry, but there is only a fuzzy vision of what that product will be. It is meant to exploit a new kind of technology, but successful products do not just exploit technology. They fill the needs of paying customers. The company should investigate the needs this new technology can fill and evaluate how valuable it will be to have a product that fills those needs.

Second, he has approved the hiring of 75 recent college graduates to work on the project. They may all be excellent engineers, but it is not clear that they have the right skills for the job, nor is it clear that 75 engineers will be needed.

There are two dangers in hiring such a large team before a product is fully described. The first is that the team may try to force the product into a shape that fits their skills rather than one that best fits customers' needs; for example, if they are all C++ coders, they may write the product in C++ even if it is not the best choice for the application. The second danger is that the team may cause the work to expand so that they stay busy, rather than simplifying the work so that the product is finished more quickly. In short, hiring a team like this may force the product to fit the skills and number of people working on it, rather than having the number of people working on it and their skills fit the needs of the product.

Applying the Scrum Framework

The Scrum framework recognizes that for any new product, two decisions must be made.

1. What should be created?
2. How should it be created?

What Should Be Created?

It makes no sense for the 75 new hires to start working until they know several things about what they are trying to produce.

For example, the executive knows he wants a product using the new technology. But what kind of product? What features should it have? What market need is it supposed to fill? The executive has talked with a few of the company's large customers and they have expressed cautious interest. They are intrigued by the idea but they want to see something tangible to evaluate before they make any commitments.

Clearly, a great deal of homework is needed. Someone needs to come up with a list of features for the new product and determine which are the most important. It may not be possible to create all the features within the six-month time frame the executive has in mind, but if any features are delivered, they must capture customers' interest.

Determining what to create is a crucial decision that involves considerable risk. Six months of work by 75 developers adds up to a large sum of money. If they deliver what they are asked to build but the product does not meet the market's needs, the initiative will be a disaster. Even worse, the company's future may be jeopardized.

As a Scrum Master, you know the new product needs a Product Owner. The Product Owner will be responsible for identifying the most valuable features to produce and prioritizing the order in which the features are created to generate the most value possible. In this way, the Product Owner would act as a kind of investor, devoting the company's time and money to produce a product of the highest possible value.

The Product Owner will also assemble and prioritize a list of goals to accomplish (or more accurately, a list of problems to solve or challenges to overcome). This prioritized list is called the Product Backlog. The Product Owner will own the product because he or she owns the Product Backlog. At any given moment, the Product Backlog will describe the vision of the finished product at that point in time.

How Should It Be Created?

In the Scrum framework, products are created by teams of people working from the items found in Product Backlogs. The teams are given full authority to manage themselves to get the work done. In return, they accept full responsibility for the results.

As a Scrum Master, you know it is important that the teams accept this responsibility, because no one else can accept it. You also know that if a team of developers is to accept responsibility for creating a product, they must be capable of creating it. In other words, the team must have all the skills and resources needed to deliver the items in the Product Backlog they agree to take on. If they don't have the skills, they cannot be held accountable for delivering the finished items. If they can only do part of the work, no one is responsible for delivering complete, finished results.

Developing a Coaching Strategy

The first thing you need to do is coach the executive to name a person to be the owner of the product and be accountable for making it valuable. Once the Product Owner is identified, he or she will spend time with the company's customers to understand what is desirable and spend time with the developers to understand what is practical and/or possible. The Product Owner will then come up with a list of features to be created and a set of priorities for doing so.

The Product Owner will also identify a set of features that will give customers something tangible to evaluate as soon as possible. This set of features is sometimes known as a minimum viable product or MVP. Producing an MVP within the six-month deadline the executive has set will be a high priority.

Once the initial Product Backlog is available, the Product Owner will need to convene a meeting in which the prioritized list is presented to the 75 newly hired developers. The purpose of the meeting will be to lay out the challenges the Product Backlog presents and start organizing the work needed to meet them.

The developers will need to organize themselves into small groups that they feel are capable of tackling individual Product Backlog items. It may become necessary to break large challenges in the Product Backlog into smaller ones that can be completed in time to be part of a periodic evaluation.

The developers should also plan to pause their work from time to time to evaluate the progress they have made and make any changes in approach that may arise. They should primarily measure the amount of actual value that has been produced. A feature only has value if it is complete, works properly, and is ready to give to a customer. The developers will have to accept responsibility for delivering value on a periodic basis, and work to make sure their efforts are coordinated in order to do so.

Development teams need to be small for their members to work together effectively. In this situation, the executive clearly expects multiple teams to be needed. Applying the Scrum framework in a multiteam setting is called scaled Scrum. There are several scaled adaptations of Scrum to choose from, including Scrum@Scale, Nexus, LeSS, and SAFe, among others.

Coaching Challenges

As the Scrum Master, you will need to tackle several coaching challenges.

Coaching the Creation of the Product Backlog

You start by working with the executive to name a Product Owner and giving him or her authority to make all decisions related to the product and its features.

When the Product Owner is named, you work with her to describe the challenges to be overcome in order to produce a valuable product. These challenges might be simple (e.g., “create a way to log in”) or complex (e.g., “create a way to evaluate a data set of arbitrary size in fewer than 100 milliseconds”). All the challenges must be posed as problems to be solved as opposed to tasks to be performed. When solved, each must have a value that can be measured.

You encourage the Product Owner to assign values to the Product Backlog items by asking potential/future customers what the relative value of each item might be. A feature or an item is only valuable if a customer is willing to pay for it. You use customer feedback extensively to understand the value of the product as it is developed and shipped.

As new Product Backlog items are identified, you coach the Product Owner to refine them with the help of developers. A valuable item is of no use if it cannot be created. You coach the Product Owner and the developers to negotiate what is desirable versus what is practical.

You also coach the Product Owner to keep an eye on the value created by the developers compared to the cost of their time and effort. The Product Owner is an investor and should be accountable for the return on the investment (ROI). There will come a time in each product's life when further investment in its development is not justifiable because of the diminishing increase in value realized. At some point, the Product Owner will have to pull the plug on the product and move the resources to other, more valuable endeavors.

Coaching the Development Teams

You work with all 75 newly hired engineers to help them realize that their job is not to perform tasks but to create a valuable product. Once they understand the challenges in the Product Backlog, they form groups to tackle them. You let each group pick the Product Backlog items they will address, recognizing that each item will be part of a product that must be a finished and working whole at the end. You make sure the teams realize they must coordinate with each other so that the features they create fit together.

You also work with the developers to identify which skills are lacking within the group. Together, you figure out how to deal with this challenge. Should more developers with the missing skills be hired? Should some existing developers be trained in the missing skills? The development team is accountable for creating the product, so the team must accept responsibility for addressing problems that impair their ability to create the product.

Finally, you teach the developers how to measure the results of their work. It is impossible to improve something if it is not measured. Without measurable results, there is no way to know whether things are getting better or worse.

Coaching Everyone

You teach everyone involved to adopt a Plan–Work–Review–Adjust cycle, known as a Sprint cycle in the Scrum framework. You start each cycle by negotiating what is to be done next, with the Product Owner emphasizing what will be valuable and the development team emphasizing what will be achievable. Then you reach an agreement on what is planned to be accomplished by the end of the upcoming cycle. In the Scrum framework, this is called the Sprint Planning meeting.

During the cycle, the development team works to deliver the agreed-upon items, identifying and overcoming obstacles as they go. The Product Owner uses this time to investigate opportunities and potentially add new items to the Product Backlog.

At the end of the cycle, everyone involved reviews the results of the work that was done and discusses the lessons that were learned. The new version of the product (incorporating the changes made during the cycle) is examined and the Product Backlog is reviewed to make sure it still describes the desired finished product. If changes to the Product Backlog are suggested, they are discussed with the Product Owner for possible inclusion. In the Scrum framework, this is called the Sprint Review.

Before the negotiation for the next cycle, it is a good idea for the Product Owner and the developers to meet and discuss any issues concerning how they are working together. If adjustments are needed, they can be included in the next cycle (known in the Scrum framework as the Sprint Retrospective).

Measuring Success

There is only one way to measure the success of a new-product development effort: by comparing the value of the product that was created to the cost of creating it.

To create value, the Product Owner and the development team depend on each other. The developers cannot create much value if the Product Owner prioritizes the wrong things for them to work on. Likewise, the Product Owner cannot create much value if the development team can only tackle the simple challenges and not the tough but valuable ones.

Conclusion

This case study involved two main challenges:

1. An urgent need but a poorly defined Product Goal
2. Hiring a large team to create the product before the size and makeup of the required team was known

To address these challenges, the following actions are recommended.

- You should coach the executive pushing the initiative to name a Product Owner and create a detailed Product Backlog, and coach the Product Owner to give high

- priority to those items that can form a minimum viable product or MVP.
- You should coach the 75 new hires to organize themselves into scaled Scrum teams to work through the items in the Product Backlog. They should be able to identify any missing skill sets and find ways to add them to the group.
- You should coach everyone to measure progress by measuring improvements to the value of the product. They need to make sure the increase in value is more than the cost of the effort to create the increase (i.e., a positive ROI).

Part II

Problems of Management and Product Ownership

Case 9:

Road Map Worries

You are a Scrum Master. You have just been hired by a small start-up that wants to start selling its app on a larger scale. Its key customers want several features developed as soon as possible. The start-up wants to use the Scrum framework to organize its efforts to leverage this opportunity.

An angel investor is funding the group for the time being. Both the group and the investor want to approach a venture capitalist for Series A financing once the company has matured a bit. The angel investor is a former chief information officer (CIO) who introduced several successful high-tech products about 10 years ago.

The angel investor is working with the young company's CEO to draw up a road map for the product's development. The road map is intended to represent a plan for the entire year, complete with milestones and deadlines.

The CEO and her team are uncomfortable with the road map. They are being asked to estimate the duration of tasks that will not be undertaken for months and whose requirements are sketchy at best.

The CEO asks you: how are road maps handled in the context of the Scrum framework?

Your assignment

1. Analyze this situation vis-à-vis the Scrum framework.

2. Come up with a strategy to deal with it.

This case illustrates a typical problem involving reconciling the realities of new-product development with an investor's need to minimize his or her perceived risk.

Initial Analysis

A product road map is a concept with roots in waterfall-style project management. A waterfall program manager maps out a series of feature enhancements that are to be created according to a fixed schedule. These enhancements are assigned to project managers who initiate and run projects to create them. The projects are sequenced according to dependencies and the expected availability of resources. When the road map is complete, it shows a comprehensive picture of planned activities, expected results, and an overall price tag for the effort.

After a draft road map is proposed, it usually goes through a review-and-revise process. This is especially true for road maps used by midsize to large organizations. Top management go through the plan in some detail and evaluate the benefit-to-cost ratio for each planned item. They make adjustments to change the timing of certain features and trim expenditures. In the end, a finalized road map is approved and given to project managers and developers to follow.

The angel investor wants such a road map for the same reason as top management in a large organization. The road map spells out a plan for delivering the new product. That means there is at least some plan that could potentially do the job. The road map also gives a definite cost for the development effort. The plan's schedule and cost allow an investor to make an informed decision about whether to invest in the effort or not.

A product road map disguises the true nature of the investment decisions involved with creating a new product. The road map makes the decision look like a simple purchase transaction. It spells out the content of a new product, its lead time, and its price. The investor can then choose to buy it as is, negotiate changes, or walk away. If the investor chooses to buy, he or she has a firm expectation that the product will be delivered according to the plan and for the agreed-upon price.

For some kinds of products, a road map can make sense. If the need the product will fill and the technology involved in creating the product are both fairly stable, it is possible to make a fairly good plan and optimize it before work begins. Building bridges and highways are examples of projects in which a product road map makes sense.

For other kinds of products, though, a road map can be very destructive. If the market for the product is evolving rapidly or the state-of-the-art techniques for creating it are advancing rapidly, a road map can cause the product to be a miss rather than a hit. A road map to produce the right product for the marketplace at the time the map was created can result in delivering the wrong product by the time development is complete.

Once a road map is approved, it becomes very hard to change. A road map describes a product that can be purchased for a set price. When the road map is approved, the stakeholders who bought it expect to see it followed. If it is not followed, the stakeholders begin to suspect that they may have been fooled. If things are not going according to plan, they worry that the product and benefits they have purchased may not end up being delivered after all.

Often, there is a very rigorous process to follow if a road map needs to be changed. There is a presumption that the original version of the road map is correct because it was reviewed and approved by all the stakeholders. Any changes have to be proven to be correct and the reason the original version was incorrect has to be carefully explained. The stakeholders must be persuaded that their original decision to approve the road map was somehow incorrect and the proposed change is needed to make the map correct again.

In practice, such product road maps are rarely changed once they are adopted. Instead, great pressure is placed on the people doing the work to both deliver and follow the plan. They are expected to meet the milestones and deadlines in the plan. They are also expected to deliver a high-quality product. It is often impossible to do both things. Since meeting a deadline is easy to measure and doing quality work is hard to measure, the tendency is for developers to take shortcuts in order to meet deadlines. This gives the appearance of success but simply piles up trouble for the future.

The crowning irony in this situation is that for most software development efforts, a formal road map is usually completely inaccurate and incorrect. Road maps are based on assumptions: the list of features that will be needed is an assumption, the amount of effort needed to create each feature is an assumption, and the availability of skilled individuals to do the work when it will be needed is an assumption. What's worse is that the people making the assumptions are not usually held accountable when the assumptions prove to be wrong.

There is an old saying: "Nothing is impossible if you don't have to do it yourself." The final fatal flaw of many product road maps is that they are formulated and approved by people who do not have to carry out the plans themselves. Those people want the illusion of certainty the road map gives them when the reality of the endeavor may be far from certain. They can cling to that illusion and focus everyone on following the plan. Following the road map can become more important than creating a valuable product.

Applying the Scrum Framework

The waterfall project model rests on assumptions of certainty, that it is possible to make predictions about future conditions and needs with a fair degree of accuracy. The Scrum framework rests on an assumption of uncertainty: nothing is certain unless it has already occurred.

The Scrum framework outlines a process of discovery. A product in Scrum is created by "discovering" how to create it. Uncertainty is gradually removed by undertaking actions and measuring the results.

The fact that the angel investor in this case study wants to create a product road map for the start-up's product reveals his current state of mind. For the angel investor, a product road map is a solution. It is worthwhile to consider what kind of problem he has, a problem he thinks a product road map will solve.

Identifying Needs

For investors to be successful, they must strike a balance between opportunity and risk. Angel investors and venture capitalists must be especially good at doing so, since the opportunities and risks they work with are so large.

The angel investor in this case study clearly wants a road map to give a sense of certainty about the product. He wants to believe there is a plan that has been carefully thought out and will lead to success if it is followed diligently. In other words, the angel investor wants to know that the risks being run are also being managed and minimized.

The angel investor is also interested in how long it will take to develop the product. He is investing his own money in the start-up. He wants to know when he can start getting it back. The idea of milestones in a road map is appealing for this reason.

So, when the angel investor asks for a road map, he is actually saying, "I want to minimize my risks and I also want to know when I can start reaping my rewards."

As Scrum Master, your job is to teach and coach the CEO and the angel investor how both needs can be met within the Scrum framework. As a matter of fact, it is difficult to meet both needs without the Scrum framework.

Maintaining and Sequencing the Product Backlog

A waterfall project plan lists tasks to be performed. A Scrum framework Product Backlog lists problems to be solved. More specifically, it lists product needs to be filled.

Rather than being sequenced by a waterfall build plan, the items in a Product Backlog are sequenced by the value of the need to be filled. In Scrum, the most valuable items in the Product Backlog are the ones to be delivered first. The developers on a Scrum Team must always be working on the most valuable Product Backlog items available at any given time.

The Scrum framework places responsibility for maintaining and sequencing the Product Backlog in the hands of the Product Owner. A Product Owner's job is to maximize the value of the work performed by the Scrum development team. He or she does so by adding product needs to the Product Backlog and sequencing them so that the most valuable ones are always at the top of the list.

At the beginning of each Sprint, the Product Owner negotiates with the development team about the Product Backlog items to be selected for delivery. In effect, the Product Owner is an investor who invests the time and efforts of the development team to produce valuable results.

As with any other investor, the success of the Product Owner can be evaluated by measuring the return on his investment in the product. If the gross return is greater than the cost of producing it, the Product Owner has made a "profit." If the product does not recover its costs, the Product Owner has incurred a "loss." The Product Owner's responsibility is to make the "profit" as large as possible.

In this case study, the angel investor is the obvious choice for the person to play the Product Owner role. He is putting up the money, after all. He is in the best position to figure out what features of the product are the most valuable and are thus worth creating.

As Scrum Master, you should work with the angel investor to create the Product Backlog. In addition to making a list of the features being requested by the customers, you should ask the angel investor to estimate the values they might represent when delivered, sequence the items so that the most valuable ones are at the top of the list, and if possible, group the valuable ones into batches that can be released to customers in a marketable way.

Once the Product Backlog has been created, it will contain a sequenced plan for developing the product. The plan will be optimized to deliver as much value as possible as early in the development process as possible. The plan will also minimize the investment risks as much as possible, as it will attempt to deliver real results as early in the process as possible.

Managing Product Backlog Changes

The Product Backlog contains a sequenced plan for developing a product just as a road map does. There is one crucial difference, though. The Product Backlog identifies priorities but does not set milestones or deadlines. It is possible to forecast potential delivery dates for specific Product Backlog items, but the actual timing of them is impossible to know. Too many things can change in the meantime.

What kinds of things can change? Just about anything.

If the market changes, it may be necessary to add new Product Backlog items or drop old ones. If the available technology changes, it may be necessary to change the priority of some Product Backlog items to take advantage of those changes. If the availability of technical talent changes, it might be necessary to adjust the sequence of development so as to maximize the value that can be delivered. It might even make sense to stop development on the product and move the resources to different pursuits if market realities call for it.

The Scrum framework is based on the principle of iteration. The Sprint cycle is designed to allow the development of the product to evolve and change on a fixed schedule. At the beginning of each Sprint, the current state of the Product Backlog is reviewed and a plan for delivering its most valuable items is negotiated. During the Sprint, while the negotiated items are being worked on, the Product Owner reviews market needs and may change the Product Backlog in any way necessary. If it turns out that drastic changes are needed, the only work that is at risk is the work of the current Sprint.

By focusing on delivering the most value possible each Sprint and by allowing plans to change on a Sprint-by-Sprint basis, the Scrum framework meets the angel investor's need to minimize his risks.

Refining the Product Backlog

Before the development team can accept the items in the Product Backlog, they have to be checked to make sure it is feasible to create them in a Sprint. The development team has to know what its capabilities are and what the sizes of the Product Backlog items are before they can agree to deliver them. For this reason, the Product Owner and the development team usually spend some time each Sprint to refine the Product Backlog items that might be selected for future Sprints.

The refining process involves the Product Owner discussing the need each Product Backlog item is meant to fill and the development team discussing technical approaches to fill that need. When everyone agrees that the need is understood and an approach is identified, the development team assigns a size to the item to be delivered. The development team compares the size of an item with its capacity to deliver items. If the item is too "large," the development team works with the Product Owner to reduce its size and/or break it into more than one valuable need to address.

The Product Backlog refining process sounds simple, but there is a major complication in the formula. How does one determine the size of a Product Backlog item? It turns out that there is no way to measure the size of an item objectively. The size cannot be measured in inches or kilograms or degrees, nor can the size of one item be compared to the size of another item in absolute terms.

The best that can be done is to use a relative unit of measure.

It is not possible to say that an item is a certain size, but it is possible to say that one item is intuitively "larger" or "smaller" than another. If there are two items, it is possible to state which one is larger. If another item is added to the list, it is possible to state that it is the smallest, the largest, or in between the other two in size. If more and more items are added in this way, they end up defining a range of sizes that can be linked to a scale.

The development team can use this scale to rank the sizes of the items in the Product Backlog. It can then work on and deliver some items and note their sizes according to this scale. After a while, the development team will have some measurements about what its capacity is. It will know the sizes of the Product Backlog items it has been able to deliver, so it has the information it needs to negotiate with the Product Owner about what it can deliver.

There are several versions of this scale of relative values. One is the story point version, with the story points typically expressed by numbers in the Fibonacci sequence (1, 2, 3, 5, 8, 13, etc.). Another is T-shirt size (XXS, XS, S, M, L, XL, XXL, XXXL, etc.). The actual scale to use doesn't matter. What matters is measuring the results of the development team's work. If a team delivered two XXLs, one M, and two XXSs, it should not agree to deliver more than two XXLs, one M, and two XXSs in the future.

The size of the Product Backlog items a development team has delivered is called its velocity. If the velocity of a development team has been measured and the sizes of the items in the Product Backlog have been estimated, it is possible to do a little math and forecast when future Product Backlog items might be delivered. If a team can deliver two XXLs per Sprint and there are nine XXLs in the Product Backlog, it is possible to forecast that work on the ninth one is likely to be started after four more Sprints.

By assigning sizes to the Product Backlog items and measuring the development team's capacity in this way, it is possible to meet the angel investor's need to know when he can start reaping his rewards.

Conclusion

The Scrum framework provides the information needed to serve the purpose of a product road map but without the associated drawbacks. It provides a clear picture of the product's development plan without limiting it to what was originally envisioned. It also provides forecasts of delivery based on the development team's measured ability to produce. As Scrum Master, you should teach and coach the angel investor to give values and priorities to Product Backlog items and coach the development team to measure its ability to deliver them.

Case 10:

Fixed-Price Contracts

You are a Product Owner at a small company. Your product is software that private medical practices use to manage physicians' cases and bill insurance providers for their work.

One day the company's vice president of sales comes into your office with exciting news: the company has a chance to sign a big contract with a medical group of more than 500 physicians. This will more than double the company's client base.

The medical group wants some customizations made to the software so that it will handle the specific needs of oncologists and their patients. According to the vice president of sales, the client is willing to cover reasonable development costs for the customizations, but has a strict requirement that the customizations be delivered within three months of signing the sales contract. When pressed about what "reasonable" development costs are, the client named a figure that is approximately equal to the salary of two skilled developers working for three months.

The vice president of sales asks you to help create a fixed-price bid for the customization work that will meet the deadline the client has imposed.

Your assignment:

1. Analyze the situation vis-à-vis the Scrum framework.

2. Figure out what to do.

This case illustrates a common dilemma software development companies face. The client has important needs and has money to pay for them to be addressed. The client wants to limit its risk, though, and insists on a firm, fixed timeline and budget. How can the company commit to a certain cost and delivery date when it is not possible to predict complications that may arise along the way?

Initial Analysis

Whenever two parties negotiate a contract, three elements must be balanced: the amount of value to be delivered, the amount of compensation to be paid for delivering that value, and the responsibility for bearing the risk of unanticipated factors and events.

If the contract involves selling an existing product, balancing the three elements is relatively cut and dried. The value of the product is known, the price is agreed to, and a warranty or disclaimer covers unexpected factors. If a warranty is offered, the seller agrees to bear responsibility for the unexpected. If the customer accepts a disclaimer, the customer agrees to assume that responsibility.

If the contract involves selling something that does not exist (or does not exist yet), the situation becomes a little more complicated. The selling of services is a good example of this kind of contract.

Service contracts generally fall into one of three categories: time and materials; cost plus; and fixed price, fixed deliverable.

In a time and materials (T&M) contract, the customer is buying the skills of the company for a fixed cost per time period. In addition, the customer agrees to reimburse the company for expenditures made on the customer's behalf. It is up to the customer to define the kind of value the company is expected to deliver during that period. It is also up to the customer to decide whether the value delivered is worth the cost.

Most importantly, though, the customer alone bears responsibility for dealing with the unexpected. Time spent is time spent, and the company is entitled to compensation for that time whether it delivers acceptable value or not.

In a cost-plus contract, the customer is buying the results the company delivers. The customer agrees to pay all costs the company has incurred plus an agreed-upon profit.

In many ways, a cost-plus contract is even worse for the customer than a T&M arrangement. The company is guaranteed a profit no matter what. The company has no incentive to minimize its costs, as the customer is obligated to pay for them regardless of how high they are. Once again, the customer bears all the risk of unexpected factors and events that prohibit the delivery of the value the customer wants.

A fixed-price, fixed-deliverable (FPFD) contract is intended to provide an arrangement that is more favorable to the customer. In an FPFD contract, the service to be delivered is spelled out in as much detail as possible. When both sides agree on the service to be provided, a fixed price is negotiated for providing that service. When the contract is signed, the company is obligated to deliver the specified service and the customer is obligated to pay the agreed-upon price.

Note that in this case, the company bears all the risk for the unexpected. The company must deliver the agreed-upon value no matter what unexpected things might get in the way.

"Fixed" Is Not Necessarily Fixed

When software is developed under an FPFD arrangement, the contract relies on many of the same assumptions used in a waterfall model. The fundamental assumptions for both are as follows.

- It is possible to precisely define the exact product to be created before any work on it begins.
- It is possible to create a detailed plan and timeline for creating that product before any work on it begins.
- Once the plan is created, all that is necessary is to follow that plan faithfully in order to deliver the required product.

These assumptions are appealing to customers because they imply that buying a service (such as development of new software) can be like buying a product: the product is defined very carefully, the plan for creating it is put together very carefully, and the plan's costs define the price tag. Everything can be settled before any work begins.

As appealing as these assumptions are, they are completely wrong. It is not possible (or even desirable) to define the product completely before work starts. It is also not possible to create a detailed plan and timeline for creating the product before work starts. Following such a plan faithfully will not guarantee delivery of the desired product.

These assumptions are false because, at the beginning of any software development project, much more is unknown about the project than is known. The customer may think they know what is required, but more than likely their understanding of their need will change as time goes on. The company may think it has created an adequate plan for developing the software, but more likely it will find out the plan needs adjustment and revision as time goes on.

Software development efforts need flexibility to deal with new and better understandings about what is needed and how to deliver it. FPFD contracts (and waterfall project plans) serve to eliminate flexibility in an effort to limit risk for the customer. Ironically, however, they introduce perhaps the greatest risk of all: the customer ends up paying for and receiving software that is what they requested but not what they need.

Applying the Scrum Framework

Products are goods and services that fill needs. In the Scrum framework, products are things that can be produced, fill needs, and have an objectively measurable value.

A Product Owner's responsibility is to guide the creation of a product so that it becomes as valuable as possible. At the beginning of each Sprint, the Product Owner identifies the needs that would be the most valuable to fill at that time. The development team selects several of those needs and agrees to fill them. They select the needs they will work on based on the size of the needs and their measured capacity to fill them.

The Product Owner maintains a list of needs to be addressed in a Product Backlog. Each need is stored as a Product Backlog item, and each item contains a description of the need, an estimate of the value that would be realized by meeting the need, and an estimate of the size of the technical challenge involved in filling the need. The Product Owner sequences the list so that the most important Product Backlog items to work on are at the top. Reading the Product Backlog from top to bottom gives a rough idea of the sequence and timeline for the delivery of specific product improvements.

The vice president of sales asks you whether it is safe to enter into an FPFD arrangement with the medical group based on the timeline and reimbursement amount they specified. Before you can answer that question, you need to know more about the customizations the client desires.

You must understand what needs the customizations are meant to address and the size of the technical challenge each one presents. It would also be helpful to know the value of each need in the eyes of the client. In short, you must add Product Backlog items for each need to the Product Backlog and understand their size as compared to the measured capacity (or velocity) of the development team to address them.

Moving from "What" to "Why"

You ask for and receive a detailed list of the customizations requested by the client. It is a long list of alterations to be made to the product's screens, reports, and database. There are instructions such as "Add the American Cancer Society diagnosis code as an input box on the patient profile screen" and "Add a checkbox to the medication screen indicating 'Experimental: approved by FDA for emergency use only'." Other changes are meant to keep track of patients who have received bone marrow transplants and whose immune systems are therefore compromised. The most complicated change is a new, long-term tracking system to follow up with patients regularly over at least five years.

You note that all of these requested changes are described in terms of "what to do." However, it is more important that you understand the purpose these changes are meant to serve. Instead of understanding *what* the client wants to have done, you need to understand *why* the client wants those things done. Understanding the "why" part is much more important than understanding the "what" part.

You arrange to meet with a representative of the medical group who oversaw the creation of the customization list. After discussing each requested change, it becomes apparent that the changes are meant to address three general needs.

1. Insurance billing: Treating cancer patients often involves special reporting requirements when requesting payment from insurance companies. Due to technology limitations, the medical group currently prepares and submits these requests by hand.
2. Malpractice insurance coverage: Treating patients with high-mortality-related conditions requires special procedures and recordkeeping to reduce the risk of malpractice lawsuits.
3. Clinical research: The medical group sees itself at the cutting edge of cancer treatment. It wants to test new therapies and understand their effects. Doing so requires special recordkeeping functionality coupled with statistical analysis tools.

You ask the representative to rate these needs in terms of their importance. The representative states that each need is very important, but if pressed to sequence them, he would put the malpractice coverage need at the top and the insurance billing need in second place; both of these are vital to the medical group's ability to stay in business. The clinical research need is a "nice to have" and is very important from the physicians' point of view. Still, lack of the clinical research piece would not bankrupt the group whereas lack of either of the other two pieces very well could do so.

After returning to your office, you add three new items to the Product Backlog.

1. As an administrator, I want the medical group to comply with the procedural and recordkeeping requirements of

2. our malpractice insurance carrier so that we are protected from lawsuits.
3. As an administrator, I want to submit payment requests for the treatment of cancer patients so that the medical group receives prompt payment of claims.
4. As a clinician, I want to track the progress of patients receiving certain treatments so that I can measure the effectiveness of those treatments.

Then you give the first item a value of “high,” the second item a value of “high,” and the third item a value of “medium to high.”

Refining the Product Backlog

During the next Product Backlog refinement session, you present the three new Product Backlog items to the development team and ask them to estimate their sizes.

The developers note that their product already has special functionality for malpractice insurance purposes; it was originally developed for the treatment of patients with HIV infections. The functionality had been removed from the user screens so that it would be invisible, but it is there. The developers note that it probably would not take much to make it visible and add any minor changes necessary to repurpose it for cancer treatment. They give this item a size of “small.”

The developers also note that the existing HIV functionality includes some hooks needed for the special insurance billing requirements those treatments impose. Those requirements involve special coding of diagnosis and pharmaceutical information to include HIV-related factors. The developers speculate that the billing of cancer treatment might have similar requirements. The difference likely involves using cancer-related factors instead of HIV-related factors in the coding. They identify two tasks for this item: research the cancer-related requirements and implement the required coding changes. The developers give this item a size of “medium.”

Finally, the developers note that the malpractice-related functionality could also be used to capture the data needed for the clinical research piece. The essence of the malpractice piece is to capture a daily diary of a patient’s condition and any treatments the patient receives. This can provide a defense in a malpractice lawsuit as it clearly shows what was done for a patient, when it was done, and why.

All that would be needed for the clinical research piece would be to understand the kinds of statistical analysis required and make or buy a statistical tool that can do the work. The developers give this item a size of “medium.”

All in all, the new Product Backlog items have sizes of “small,” “medium,” and “medium.” Looking at the history of the development team, over the past 12 Sprints they were able to complete an average of three “small” and two “medium” items each Sprint. The length of a Sprint for this team was two weeks, so you can feel very confident that the client’s needs will be met within its three-month time frame.

Making the Deal

Based on the information gained through the Product Backlog refinement process, you talk about the situation with the vice president of sales. You propose that she make a counteroffer to the client. She should ask the client to purchase the base product and fund 50% of the cost of one Sprint for the Scrum Team. Fifty percent of the cost of a Sprint would represent approximately one-third of the “reasonable” amount the client was willing to pay for the customizations. In return, you promise to show a rough draft of the functionality needed after only two weeks.

When the two-week Sprint is finished, the representative will be invited to come and view for himself what has been accomplished. At that point, he can correct any misunderstandings and/or make suggestions about further changes. If any are required, the client can decide to fund 50% of the next Sprint and see the results again after another two weeks. This process can continue until the client is satisfied that the software meets its needs.

After some further discussion, the vice president of sales proceeds to draw up a formal proposal along the lines you have recommended. The proposal is presented to the client, and after some discussions, the client agrees.

The first Sprint takes place and the representative is invited to join the Sprint Review. He is very impressed. The malpractice and clinical research pieces are there and are working properly.

The developers note that some of the research they did shows that they underestimated the complexity of the insurance billing requirements for cancer patients. After talking with some major insurance providers, they nailed down the actual data elements needed and are ready to build them into the product. This functionality is not available to be demonstrated at this Sprint Review but will be ready soon. They ask the representative to please be patient and thank him for his understanding.

The representative is very enthusiastic about the progress that has been made. He says he looks forward to the insurance billing piece being completed.

At the same time, he notes that the costs so far have left some unused funds in his budget. Could they perhaps be used to make some further changes?

When asked what he has in mind, the representative notes that all the screens used by the physicians and nurses are optimized for use on a laptop. Sometimes it is not convenient to leave a patient's bedside to use a laptop to record a treatment entry. Would it be possible to allow the clinicians to use a smartphone instead?

The developers reply that it would be difficult to build a smartphone version of all the system's screens, but if all that was required would be to allow the recording of patient conditions and treatments in the patient diary, that would not be a very big deal.

You add an item to the Product Backlog that states, "As a nurse or physician, I want the flexibility to record a patient's condition and any treatment administered using a smartphone so that I do not have to leave the patient's bedside to record this information on a laptop."

The representative is very enthusiastic about the Sprint Review and about the progress made. He comments that he will ask his team if there are any other enhancements that might be helpful. He implies that he will try to find funding for them if necessary.

Conclusion

FPFD contracts are intended to eliminate risk for a customer trying to purchase new software. However, they prevent flexibility and often lead to situations in which the software does what the customer thought they wanted but does not address the customer's underlying need.

The Scrum framework provides more safety and less risk by limiting the amount of time between starting work and showing results. Something that is complete and "done" must be delivered by the end of every Sprint. Stated another way, every Sprint must produce something that has measurable value. That result is inspected in the Sprint Review and adjustments to the Product Backlog can be made. The customer (through the Product Owner) can ask for changes in direction, or even pull the plug if the review shows results that are not acceptable. All that is at risk is the cost of two weeks' worth of time and effort. This risk is small compared to the benefit of being able to adjust and correct the course of the work in order to get the right product in the end.

The final product might not be what the customer originally asked for, but it is very likely to be what the customer actually needs.

Case 11:

Dealing with the Director of Engineering

You are a Scrum Master, and you have been assigned to help a team that is not performing to expectations.

The company's director of engineering recently assumed leadership of the team, and he is attempting to manage the team and organize its members. The team goes through the motions of following the Scrum events, but the director of engineering is exercising "command and control" tactics, so the Scrum events have little practical value. He decides the scope of each Sprint, assigns tasks to the developers on the team, and then tracks their progress. He also performs most of the architectural and design tasks, and he gives detailed instructions to the developers to follow when performing their work.

The director of engineering has just been notified that he is being promoted. He will soon be vice president of engineering.

You have been assigned to this team at the director's request. Before you join the team, he takes you aside and explains that he wants your help with something. He identifies two individuals on the development team and says they are "special." He wants you to coach them to become effective development leads. He confides that he wants to split the team into two groups and wants you to teach the new leads how to become the managers of the new teams.

Your assignment:

1. Analyze this situation vis-à-vis the Scrum framework.

2. Come up with a plan of action for proceeding with the new situation.

This case illustrates a common dilemma facing many Scrum Masters. They are asked to help straighten out teams that are not performing well, but management expects them to subvert the use of the Scrum framework in order to do so.

Initial Analysis

As the Scrum Master, you need to research the history of the problem team so that you understand why they are perceived to be underperforming. If you discover that there is a problem, you must come up with an approach that will solve it. Once a strategy is in place, you will need to persuade the director of engineering that the new approach is correct and will be effective.

This may take some careful persuasion, as you realize the director has his own plan. He has been implementing his command-and-control model, but without much success. Now he wants you to follow his plan and even teach two developers how to be command-and-control-type managers. You note that charging you with implementing his plan lets him avoid any responsibility for the results. If things go well, he can claim credit. If things do not go well, he can blame you for not carrying out his instructions properly.

After some research and some interviews with various people, you realize that the team's poor performance has to do with their inability to meet deadlines.

The company's top management publishes an annual road map for new-product development. This road map sets certain milestones that must be met on a quarterly basis. Several development teams are working on this road map and all of them have missed at least one milestone this year. The team you have been assigned to fix has missed most of its milestones, having completed only about 30% of them on time so far.

Top management is worried that the road map may not be completed on schedule. The director of engineering told them he would “kick some butt” and take care of the problem. He took control of the team, parceled out assignments to its members, pushed them hard, and told them they had to get the work finished on time “or else.” The result: the team reported that the next set of milestones was met, top management was relieved, and the director was promoted to vice president of engineering.

Studying the Development Team

As the Scrum Master, you determine that the best place to start is to see what has been going on and get a feel for how the development team works together. So you decide to observe a few initial Scrum events without trying to influence them just yet.

Your first discovery is that the team is large. There are 15 people in the room during the first Daily Scrum that you attend. Each person in turn gives answers to the three traditional Daily Scrum questions.

- What have you done since the last Daily Scrum?
- What will you have done by the next Daily Scrum?
- What is blocking progress, if anything?

The director of engineering asks the questions and the team answers. There is almost no discussion at all.

You find that the team keeps a set of burn-down charts of their progress. Each developer on the team has a separate chart showing the status of his or her assignments. The director tells each developer they are expected to bring their chart to 100% completion by the end of each Sprint.

You also find that the team conducts a Sprint Planning meeting at the beginning of each Sprint and a Daily Scrum each day. They do not, however, conduct a Sprint Review or a Sprint Retrospective.

The Sprint Planning meeting consists of the director of engineering giving assignments to the various developers. They are expected to ask any questions necessary to make sure they understand the tasks they have been given. At the end of the meeting, they are asked to acknowledge their assignments and verbally commit to getting them done.

There is no Sprint Review, because the director says it is not necessary. The developers have their assignments and must complete them. The only thing to review is whether the assignments are complete or not. That information is available from the burn-down charts.

Finally, you discover that the Sprint Retrospective was held a few times and then the practice was discontinued. Very little was discussed when it was held and everyone felt it was a waste of time.

Assessing Developer Morale

You are worried that the pressure being applied by the director of engineering might hurt the development team's morale. After a few one-on-one talks with some team members, it becomes clear that morale is fine. The developers don't like getting pushed, but they found ways to satisfy the director's needs. Once they did that, he pretty much left them alone.

They also liked the fact that their only responsibilities were to do the tasks the director assigned to them. The trick was to avoid being assigned tasks that were too tedious or difficult to do. They learned that if they complained loudly about the workload they were being given, the director would feel he was being tough. He was happy as long as he felt he was hard on the developers. They were happy when they convinced him he was being hard even though the assignments weren't very hard at all.

In the beginning, the director had forced the developers to work hard to catch up to where they should have been according to the road map. They caught up by working quickly and taking shortcuts. They knew that most of their catch-up work was of poor quality and would have to be redone later. They didn't worry, though, because the director obviously cared more about meeting deadlines than about putting out a quality product.

The developers even found ways to avoid trouble when deadlines were missed. The most important thing to do when a delivery could not be made on time was to figure out who could be blamed. A favorite tactic was to give a half-finished item to the testing people the day before the item was due. When the deadline came and the item was not available, the coder would say it was being tested, implying that the testers were slow. When the tests revealed serious functional problems, the coder would say the testers found the bugs too late for the coder to fix by the deadline. This would usually satisfy the director and he would turn his attention elsewhere.

After concluding your initial analysis, you understand that both the director of engineering and the development team need help. The director is focused on meeting deadlines, and the developers are focused on performing tasks and complaining about how difficult they are. No one is focused on what really matters: delivering value.

Applying the Scrum Framework

The Scrum framework provides a structure for organizing the creation of valuable products. It focuses on creating value for a very simple reason. Developing new products requires investing considerable amounts of time and money. Those investments only make sense if the value of the created product is greater than the cost of creating it. For a Scrum Team to be successful, there must be a positive return on that investment (ROI). The team must produce more value than it consumes.

Normally, a Scrum development team works from a list of items contained in a Product Backlog. A Product Backlog is a list of valuable things a Scrum development team can do and is sequenced in such a way as to maximize the value it can create. During the Sprint Planning meeting, the development team and the creator of the Product Backlog (the Product Owner) negotiate an agreed-upon scope for the upcoming Sprint. The development team selects items from the Product Backlog to work on and deliver. The Product Owner makes sure the value of the items to be delivered is enough to offset the cost of having the development team deliver them.

Normally, a well-constructed Product Backlog and a properly conducted Sprint Planning meeting cause everyone involved to focus on delivering value. The Sprint Review event is also used to confirm the value of the work actually delivered and identify other valuable opportunities that might become future Product Backlog items. The Sprint Retrospective is used to let the Scrum Team examine how well it was able to create value and identify opportunities to improve its ability to do so.

Avoiding Shortcuts

One of the hidden problems to deal with here is the presence of technical debt. Technical debt is work that is "owed" to the product because of hasty work done or shortcuts taken in the past. It is clear to you that one way the director of engineering got the team caught up to the road map milestones was by pressuring them into creating technical debt.

Technical debt in general is usually the result of applying pressure to meet deadlines. The Scrum framework uses two strategies to minimize the pressure to take shortcuts.

The first strategy is to prevent the imposition of deadlines. The Scrum development team is literally its own boss. At the beginning of each Sprint, it selects the work it will do from the list of Product Backlog items. No one can force the team to accept work it does not select itself. Also, the deadline is clear and no one can change it after the team makes its selection. By the end of the Sprint Planning meeting, the development team has selected the challenges it will face. The only pressure they might feel is pressure they place on themselves.

The second strategy is to make it very clear what it means for a Product Backlog item to be finished. Generally speaking, a Product Backlog item is finished when it can be delivered for use by a customer with no further work required. To avoid ambiguity and misunderstanding about what "no further work required" means, the Scrum framework uses a formal Definition of Done to make clear what details must be addressed before no further work is required.

Allowing the Scrum development team to select its own workload removes any motivation to deliberately add technical debt to a product. The Definition of Done serves to prevent the addition of technical debt through carelessness. It usually consists of a kind of checklist of things to verify before releasing a product feature. Following are some examples of checklist items.

- Has the programming been peer reviewed?
- Have installation instructions been written and tested?
- Has the spelling of all words visible to the end user been checked?
- Has the appearance of all user interface panels been checked on all the supported browsers?

The Definition of Done usually grows as the Scrum Team gets more experience developing the product. Every time something slips through to the end user, a preventive entry is added to the Definition of Done checklist.

Making a Product Backlog Out of a Road Map

The Scrum framework assigns responsibility for maintaining a Product Backlog to a Product Owner. A Product Owner is responsible for maximizing the value of the owned product. He or she does so by identifying valuable additions or changes to make to the product. These changes are put into the Product Backlog and sequenced in order to create the most value possible. The Product Owner then works with the development team to create the items in the Product Backlog and realize the value they represent.

As the Scrum Master, you are in a tricky situation. What is the product? Who owns it? What is the Product Backlog? All you really have is the product development road map published by top management.

The road map is not a Product Backlog. It is a list of tasks and deadlines. Those tasks and deadlines are meant to mesh together in order to create a valuable whole when they are finished. The finished product is not directly described.

Your job in this case is to get the details in the road map peeled back in order to understand the purpose they are intended to serve. It is not unlike looking at a pile of chips and circuit boards in order to understand the beautiful cell phone they are supposed to become. In Scrum, the focus must be on the end product and its value, not the steps that might be required to create it.

The essence of the Scrum framework is the coupling of responsibility with capability/competence. Decisions must be made by individuals who are capable of making them well. In exchange for this authority, those individuals accept responsibility for the results of those decisions.

The creation of a road map for teams to work against is an investment decision. The creators of the road map are investing time and money in order to have it followed. They end up being evaluated based on the return on that investment.

The role the creators of the road map play is identical to the role of a Scrum framework Product Owner. The creators of the road map identified a set of valuable things to create and worked with someone to create a plan and a schedule for creating them. A Product Backlog is a list of those valuable things but without a plan or a schedule. Instead, the Product Backlog items are sequenced according to their value. They will be created according to that sequence, with the most valuable ones created first.

After completing this analysis, you meet with top management, explain the role of the Product Owner, and ask them to name one for the team to work with. After the Product Owner is identified, you work with her to create a Product Backlog that describes the valuable results the road map was intended to create.

Coaching the Development Team

The Scrum framework calls for the development team to manage itself in order to create the value identified in the Product Backlog items. To do so, they must be cross-functional, which means they must have all the skills needed to create the product. Once again, this is an example of Scrum's coupling of responsibility and competence. If a team does not have the ability to create a product, they cannot be held accountable for doing so. If a team can create a product and undertakes to do so, they must have complete authority to manage the work or else they cannot be blamed for bad results.

One tricky aspect of this situation is that the development team is not used to accepting responsibility. They have gotten used to being told what to do. All they have had to worry about is doing the tasks they have been assigned. Whether and how much the task adds to the value of the resultant product is someone else's problem, not theirs.

You can set them straight by coaching them. You can start by saying they are now free to make their own decisions about the work they do. No more deadlines imposed by the director of engineering or anyone else. They are free to do as they please.

At the same time, they have to be mindful of the value of the work they choose to do. If they choose to do little of value, they will soon find out that the company is no longer interested in paying them. Every hour they spend working for the company represents an investment that is expected to have a positive return. If their work does not return enough value (or any at all), the company will find another way to invest its money.

At the beginning of each Sprint, there is a negotiation between the Product Owner and the development team about how much value is to be delivered. This negotiation is known as the Sprint Planning meeting and its result is an agreed-upon scope for the work of the upcoming Sprint. The Product Owner argues for creating the most value possible. The development team argues for doing only what is possible. In the end, they reach a compromise that satisfies the Product Owner and the developers. The Product Owner gets enough value to satisfy the return on the investment and the developers get a manageable workload and items they can deliver.

What About the Two "Special" Developers?

The last piece of the puzzle you must deal with is the director of engineering's desire for you to be a mentor for two promising developers. The director wants you to help them become team managers. He wants you to help them grow.

You have a dilemma. How can you help these people become team managers when the Scrum framework contains no such title or position?

To solve this dilemma, you talk with the individuals to find out what their ambitions are.

It turns out that one of them is an exceptional technical talent that the director of engineering wants to reward with a promotion. The other one is interested in understanding teams and helping people work well together.

You advise the technical person to focus on understanding and increasing his knowledge of technology. He can also play a role in training and mentoring more junior people if he so desires, but his best contribution would be to improve the technical excellence of the product. He should continue to be a developer.

You advise the other person to consider studying the Scrum framework. Your role is almost completely focused on helping teams of people work well together. If this person wants to grow in that direction, you offer her the chance to take on some of your duties for the team.

Conclusion

The Scrum framework focuses on the delivery of value rather than the execution of tasks against deadlines. Moving from a traditional to a Scrum-based approach involves de-emphasizing the measurement of activity and emphasizing the measurement of results.

Case 12:

Monitoring Work-from-Home Developers

You are an Agile Coach, and you work for a company that sells industry-leading data center management software. With the onset of the COVID-19 pandemic, companies began asking their employees to work from home to curb the spread of the coronavirus. As a result, business is booming for your company: the increased use of online video conferencing software and other tools is putting a strain on existing infrastructure, and your company's software helps manage that strain.

The head of software development at your company asks you to help solve a problem. The company is moving to an online, work-from-home model for its software developers. The development head is worried that if his developers don't have to come to the office, they may slack off. He has explored several technical tools for monitoring the developers, including a tool that counts the keystrokes of logged-in developers and one that registers when they log in and log out each day.

The development head wants to know whether there are Agile metrics he can use to make sure the developers are working hard. He is used to seeing his people put in 10-hour days and six-day weeks. He feels everyone should be busy all the time. He wants to make sure they stay busy even if they work from home.

Your assignment:

1. Analyze the situation vis-à-vis the Scrum framework.
2. Give advice and/or guidance to the head of software development.

This case illustrates some misconceptions about managing technical people engaged in the development of new products.

Initial Analysis

The development head in this case study is an old-school manager who started as a coder more than 20 years ago and worked his way up to his present leadership position. He attributes his advancement to his willingness to always go the extra mile when carrying out assignments. He works hard, routinely putting in 10-hour days and six-day weeks. He expects those under him to do the same.

He developed his management style by reading about the "management by walking around" technique made famous by Hewlett-Packard co-founders Bill Hewlett and Dave Packard. He prefers his people to work in an open space where he can wander around and see what they are doing. He cannot necessarily see what they are typing on their keyboards, but he can see whether they are concentrating on their work or not.

The development head strictly prohibits actions he characterizes as "goofing off." For example, private phone calls are forbidden, as are web browsing and the use of social media. Internet access from within the internal network is carefully controlled via the corporate firewall. No outside sites are accessible unless the department head has approved them.

The workday starts promptly at 8:30 a.m. Developers are expected to be at their desks and ready to start work at that time. They are allowed two 15-minute breaks: one mid-morning and one mid-afternoon. They are allowed a 30-minute lunch break and are encouraged to spend it in the company cafeteria. At 7:30 p.m., the developers are free to go home, but the department head makes no secret of the fact that he likes people to stay even later than that on occasion.

Developers are expected to put in a full day's work over the weekend, but whether they do it on Saturday or Sunday is up to them. The company recognizes that there are religious and family-related considerations that make it inappropriate to require attendance on a particular day of the weekend.

One reason the development head requires such long hours is that none of the developers are subject to overtime rules. Some are contractors and some are company employees, but all of them earn a large enough hourly rate that they are exempt from the laws that would require extra pay for work in excess of eight hours per day or 40 hours per week. The contractors are also expected to only request payment for a "professional eight-hour day." In other words, they are expected to receive payment for only eight hours per day no matter how many hours they work.

The only acceptable reason for a developer not to be at his or her desk is that he or she is in a problem-solving meeting. There are lots of problems to solve, and lots of these meetings are held all the time. Some software architects and functional leads spend almost 100% of their time in these meetings. Some people privately complain that the only time they are productive is when they are commuting to and from the office.

While the department head has always put in long hours, developers were not always required to do so. Two years ago, the company's stakeholders started to complain about poor results from the software development efforts. There seemed to be lots of activity, yet there was very little to show for it. At first, staffing was increased to address the problem, but this tactic caused a decrease in results. Ultimately, the 10-hour/six-day model was instituted. The 10/6 model initially led to some improvement, but the improvement was not sustainable.

The department head has been perplexed for some time. When he wanders around, he sees a buzz of activity. Everyone is busy working on something, and many problem-solving meetings occur every day. Despite all this activity, though, the stakeholders continue to be unhappy with the results.

The COVID-19 Crisis

Things truly took a turn for the worse with the onset of the COVID-19 pandemic in the spring of 2020. The company is located in the San Francisco Bay Area, and the lockdown rules that came into effect required that all the developers work from home. They no longer worked in the open space in which the department head could wander around. They no longer were required to start their day at 8:30 a.m. and work until 7:30 p.m. There was no way to monitor their 15-minute mid-morning and mid-afternoon breaks or their 30-minute lunch break. There was no way to block access to web browsing or forbidden Internet locations. There was no longer a way for the department head to tell at a glance who was working hard and who was not.

All the standard tools the department head used to measure development activity had become unavailable practically overnight. He was desperate to find some Agile metrics that would take their place.

Applying the Scrum Framework

When the Scrum framework is used properly, software is created by cross-functional, self-managing teams of developers. They work from a prioritized list of needs the product should fill. This list is called the Product Backlog.

The Product Backlog is managed and maintained by a person known as the Product Owner. The Product Owner's job is to add valuable needs to the Product Backlog list. Each need (known as a Product Backlog item) has a description of what is needed, a rating of how valuable filling it would be, and another rating of how big a technical challenge it would be to fill it.

A Product Owner must estimate the value of each Product Backlog item so that he or she can make rational decisions about when the development team should try to fill the need it represents. Generally speaking, the Product Owner wants a development team to work on the most valuable Product Backlog items it can at all times.

Scrum framework development teams must be cross-functional. This means the teams must be able to create the product they are working on without outside help. They must also be self-managing, which means they must make their own decisions about how to make the product. Both characteristics are required for a development team to accept responsibility for delivering a product.

For a development team to be able to work together and make its own decisions, it must be small enough to do so. The Scrum framework calls for teams of no more than 10 people. Larger teams than that usually have trouble coordinating their efforts effectively. Scrum works best when a few capable people with the right mix of skills can focus on needs described in Product Backlog items and fill them.

Classic Scrum describes a way for a single development team to organize itself to deliver a product. If the number of developers available is more than can fit on a single team, there are several scaled Scrum frameworks that can be used.

The main challenge any scaled Scrum framework must address is inter-development team dependency. If the work of one team depends on the completion of another team's work, there is a dependency between those teams. Likewise, if more than one team requires the help of a single expert with a special skill, there is a dependency between those teams.

The Scrum framework principle of self-management applies to large groups of developers working on the same product. They review the needs expressed in the Product Backlog items and select the items they will undertake to complete. Then they break into small, cross-functional teams capable of delivering individual, finished solutions. To the extent that there are any dependencies to worry about, they monitor the status of those dependencies on a daily basis, and intervene if necessary.

Scrum framework development teams manage themselves. There is no role for an outside manager to direct them to do anything. They set their own work hours, their own work rules, and their own internal responsibilities. If they choose to work only four hours per day and three days per week, no one can tell them they cannot do so. They are their own bosses.

Being one's own boss does not mean having no responsibility at all. On the contrary, being the boss places the heaviest possible burden onto one's shoulders. The boss is not accountable for activity. The boss is accountable for results.

A self-managing development team is able to organize itself any way it wants to. No one can hold it accountable for the way it operates. At the same time, a self-managing, cross-functional development team cannot escape accountability for the results it produces.

Each Product Backlog item has a value that has been estimated by the Product Owner. That value can be checked when the Product Backlog item's need has been filled and its benefit has been measured. It takes only some simple math to find out whether a development team produces more value than it costs to keep it in place. If a development team produces more than it costs, all is well. If it costs more than it produces, it is time to get rid of that team and get a new one.

Measuring Value, Not Activity

There is an old truism in the management world: "You get what you measure." If, as a manager, you rely on a certain key statistic to evaluate your subordinates, they will make sure they measure up well in that way.

The department head in this case study makes it clear that he cares about activity. He wants to make sure his people are busy all the time. They realize this and make sure they stay busy all the time. They focus on being busy rather than on producing results.

The onset of the COVID-19 crisis may have been a blessing in disguise for the department head. Since he is no longer able to measure how busy his people are, he will be forced to measure the only thing that can be measured: the results his people produce.

Transforming the Workplace

The first step needed to switch from an activity-based management paradigm to a results-based paradigm is to figure out how to quantify those results. In the Scrum framework, needs are recorded and prioritized in the Product Backlog. Each item in the Product Backlog describes a particular need to be filled and an estimate of the value that filling the need will produce. To focus on results rather than activity, the company must create a Product Backlog for each of its products. A development team's effectiveness can be measured by the amount of value contained in the Product Backlog items it delivers.

You suggest working (via a video conferencing tool) with the stakeholders to create the necessary Product Backlogs. At least one stakeholder is especially interested in each product being developed. These stakeholders have the authority to make funding decisions for those products. They are also in touch with key customers who are interested in those products.

After meeting with you, the stakeholders agree to play the role of Product Owner for their respective products. With your help, they create a number of Product Backlog items, estimate their value, and prioritize them in a way designed to produce the most value.

Next, you e-mail all the developers, asking them to choose a product to work on. You convene an online meeting for each product team during which the Product Owner presents the Product Backlog to the developers. Each Product Backlog item is discussed and adjusted according to the technical challenges the developers foresee. When everyone is satisfied that at least the first few Product Backlog items are well understood, the developers agree to undertake several of them and to deliver results in two weeks.

After the Product Owner and the developers have agreed on what is to be delivered, the developers break into small teams to tackle individual Product Backlog items. Each team has all the skills and abilities needed to deliver a "done" Product Backlog item, and they accept responsibility for doing so. To the extent that dependencies between teams exist, they take steps to manage and mitigate them.

At the end of the two-week period, the teams get together and show the results of their work. They demonstrate to the Product Owner/stakeholder the newly created version of the product. A discussion of next steps ensues and the Product Backlogs are updated accordingly.

At your suggestion, the total amount of value delivered is published. In addition, the contributions to that value from each team are also published. The total value delivered provides a benchmark that future results can be compared against. The teams can compare their contributions so that each team understands where their results are strong and where they may be weak. The development group can engage in some friendly competition about which team delivers the most value. They can also take steps to strengthen the weak areas.

Conclusion

Measuring activity is often incorrectly assumed to be a measurement of results. In fact, measuring activity provides only a measurement of activity. Activity may or may not be useful. If management wants everyone to be busy, subordinates will make sure they remain busy at all times. If necessary, they will invent busywork to do. This can take the form of complicated documentation requirements, complex authorization and sign-off procedures, and multilevel reviews by multiple technical authorities.

As the process becomes more complicated, the effort becomes more disorganized. When results start to decrease, the first impulse is often to add staff. Adding staff is possibly the worst thing to do. Adding more people to an already disorganized effort will only make it more disorganized. All those new people (who quickly learn that they are expected to remain busy all the time) will soon create even more busywork to do.

Managers often rely on measuring activity for one simple reason: activity is easy to measure. The department head in this case study could measure the activity of his people simply by watching them.

The Scrum framework emphasizes that measuring activity is utterly unimportant. Activity does not matter. Value matters. The Scrum framework focuses everyone on producing and measuring value.

The activity of a team with members working from their homes cannot be measured. Nor should it be. The only thing it makes sense to measure is the value a team produces. That value can be measured precisely no matter where the team members do their work.

Case 13:

Coaching an Aggressive Senior Product Owner

You are an Agile Coach charged with helping your client perform a company-wide Agile transformation.

A newly promoted senior Product Owner barged into a recent Sprint Planning meeting, taking over from the junior Product Owner the Scrum Master had been working with. The senior Product Owner was promoted because of his aggressive approach and his perceived ability to “get things done.”

According to the Scrum Master, the senior Product Owner proceeded to throw out all the story point values the team had assigned to the Sprint’s stories. Then he told the team to use a scale based on the estimated duration of each task and bullied them into providing low estimates for each Product Backlog item.

As a result of this estimation process, the team’s velocity dropped from approximately 100 story points per Sprint to roughly 40 story points per Sprint.

The senior Product Owner then told the Scrum Master he expected her to bring the team’s velocity back up to 100 points.

The Scrum Master has asked you for help.

Your assignment:

1. Analyze the situation vis-à-vis the Scrum framework.

2. Formulate a plan of action.

This case illustrates a common misunderstanding of story points and an equally common misunderstanding of the role of the Scrum Product Owner.

This company is trying to move away from a waterfall development model and adopt an Agile model instead. The senior Product Owner in this case is a former senior program manager for the company. He sees his role as putting pressure on people to meet deadlines. Although he was promoted to be a "senior program manager", he has adopted the title of senior Product Owner because that is what he believes Agile calls for. He is trying to play the role he knows best and assumes a senior Product Owner is basically a senior program manager operating under a different title.

The senior Product Owner is attempting to put pressure on the developers and the Scrum Master to improve performance. He bullies the team into making distorted estimates of story points, and when the team's velocity is reduced as a result, he pressures everyone to bring velocity back up to what it was before he intervened.

The senior Product Owner mistakenly believes that all software is of equal value, and so it makes sense to press developers to make as much of it as possible. He also mistakenly believes that story points are a measure of software quantity. He thinks, "The more story points delivered, the better."

Initial Analysis

The role of Product Owner (senior or otherwise) is fundamentally different from that of program manager. A program manager assembles resources to formulate and follow a detailed plan. The program manager's primary responsibility is to make sure the plan is followed and deadlines are met (or exceeded). Success is measured by how closely the plan is followed and whether the work is completed on time and under budget.

A Product Owner, in contrast, is not concerned about plans and deadlines. A Product Owner's job is to guide the developers in creating as much value as possible. He or she does so by identifying the most valuable things they should be working on at any given time. Success is not measured in terms of being on time or under budget. Success is measured by how much value is produced. A Product Owner's success is measured based on how much value is created compared to the cost of creating it (otherwise known as return on investment or ROI).

It makes no sense to bully developers into delivering large pieces of software that have little value. Focusing on story points causes developers to try to maximize their efforts. They may choose to work on "large" Product Backlog items that have little value rather than smaller ones that have great value.

The Scrum Product Owner role calls for an understanding of how to measure the value of the product that is owned. The Product Owner makes choices about how to increase the value of the product. The Product Owner invests the time and resources of the development team to do so. The success of the Product Owner can be measured by the return on that investment.

Another downside of pressuring developers to deliver too quickly is the effect such pressure has on the quality of the product. Developers who try to work too quickly take shortcuts and make mistakes. Over time, these shortcuts and mistakes add up, making the product unreliable and hard to maintain. The accumulation of these shortcuts and mistakes is called technical debt. In effect, it is work that is "owed" to the product.

Technical debt must be repaid. Otherwise, the product will become increasingly unreliable and the costs of making changes to it will continue to grow.

The main challenge for any Agile Coach in this situation is to teach the senior Product Owner to focus on measuring and improving product value. Bullying developers into working "harder" is irrelevant and counterproductive.

Applying the Scrum Framework

Within the Scrum framework, a Product Owner is only a Product Owner if that person "owns" a product. Owning a product means accepting responsibility for the value of the product. A Product Owner's job is to devise ways to measure the value of the product and identify ways to increase that value.

There is no such role as senior Product Owner within the Scrum framework. A person either owns a product or does not. Individual companies may choose to give the "senior" distinction to Product Owners who own particularly valuable products or who spend time mentoring less experienced Product Owners. The waterfall model distinguishes between project managers (who manage individual product improvement efforts) and program managers (who manage sets of projects to improve products). The Scrum framework makes no such distinction.

As the Agile Coach in this case study, the first thing you should do in applying the Scrum framework is figure out what the product is. Sometimes identifying the correct product can be tricky.

In this case study, the company provides online financial services. It has a main website plus Android and iPhone apps. Its customers are ordinary individuals who log in to perform various financial transactions. The company makes money by charging fees for these services.

So, the question is, what is the product? Also, is there only one product or are there several of them? And what makes something a product?

In the Scrum framework, a product is something that can be produced and has an objectively measurable value. The value must be measurable or else there is no way to maximize it. A Product Owner's job is to maximize the production of value, so a Scrum product is something that can be made and has a yardstick by which to measure whether its value is increasing or not.

The value of the main website can be tracked by measuring the transaction revenue it produces. Likewise, the Android and iPhone app transaction revenues can be measured. Transaction revenue from the various individual financial services can also be measured. There are many possible choices.

One complication is that the website and the apps rely on the services of an online back-end transaction engine. Is this back-end engine a product?

Arguments can be made that the back-end engine is a component and not a product, and that its value depends on the value of the customer-facing parts of the system. It can also be argued that the back-end engine's value can be measured by tracking the value of the transactions it processes. In any event, changes and improvements to the back-end engine should be prioritized based on their effect on value, and someone who accepts responsibility for maximizing value should make those decisions.

This company has chosen to regard the main website, the Android and iPhone apps, and the back-end engine as separate products. Each has a Product Owner, Scrum Master, and one or more development teams assigned to it. The Product Owners for these different products are relatively junior-level people who used to be waterfall-style product managers. They now report to the senior Product Owner.

Accountability Is the Key

Within the Scrum framework, there is a basic trade-off. People who are competent to make decisions about things are given unlimited and absolute authority to do so. In exchange, they accept unlimited and absolute responsibility for the results of those decisions. When the results are bad, only they are accountable. The "magic" that makes Scrum work so well is this alignment of authority, responsibility, and capability coupled with measurement tools to make the results of decisions transparent.

When the senior Product Owner barged into the Sprint Planning meeting and forced everyone to accept his decisions, he may have thought he was making those people feel accountable for carrying out his directives. In fact, the opposite was true. He was relieving everyone else of any accountability at all.

When people make their own decisions, they have no choice. They must accept accountability for the results of those decisions. When people are given directions to follow, they feel little or no accountability for the results.

If they follow the directions successfully, there is no problem. If they cannot follow the directions successfully, they feel it is not necessarily their fault. After all, the directions might have been wrong or the tasks might have been too hard to be reasonable. They can point fingers at the person giving the directions.

Likewise, the person giving the directions feels no accountability for the results. There is an old saying: "Nothing is impossible if you don't have to do it yourself." When people give orders, they disconnect themselves from actually producing the desired results. They can point fingers at the people who were supposed to follow those orders. If bad results happen, the temptation is to assume the people given the orders were not competent to carry them out properly.

Maximizing Value

The heart of the Scrum framework is the Sprint Planning meeting. During this meeting, the Product Owner and the developers negotiate and agree on a plan to deliver the most value possible during the upcoming Sprint. The Product Owner presents a list of choices about what would be valuable to work on. The development team chooses items from the list based on their estimated capacity to get them done. In the end, they all agree on a scope. Since everyone agrees, they all own the decision and the results that flow from it. They have no one to blame but themselves if things don't work out as expected.

The senior Product Owner has no business being part of the Sprint Planning negotiation. His presence will only serve to distract and disrupt. If worse comes to worst, he will allow the real Product Owner and the development team to avoid reaching an agreement that they all own.

An experienced Scrum Master would recognize this danger and (politely) tell the senior Product Owner to go away.

You, as an Agile Coach, can coach the Scrum Master to be more assertive in protecting the team from this kind of intrusion.

Also, as an Agile Coach, you can go to the senior Product Owner and coach him on more effective ways to get better results.

Making Investment Decisions

In coaching the senior Product Owner, you would make points about the relationship between accountability, responsibility, and capability within the Scrum framework. He needs to understand that by trying to pressure people to produce results, he is actually letting them all off the hook.

You can also help the senior Product Owner understand the importance of measuring the value produced as opposed to the level of effort made during a Sprint. Remember the old truism: "Management gets what it measures." If management only measures how busy people are, everyone will make sure they stay busy all the time whether they are doing something useful or not. Only if management measures the value of people's work product will they get everyone focused on delivering value.

As previously stated, a Product Owner is an investor. He or she makes "bets" on which product improvements will be most valuable. The Product Owner should measure the actual increase in the product's value once the improvements have been made. This provides feedback the Product Owner can learn from in order to make better bets in the future.

As the manager of the junior Product Owners under him, the senior Product Owner should help his people learn how to measure product value. He should help his people learn how to identify opportunities to exploit, help them prioritize them, and then understand their effect on product value after they have been implemented.

In short, the senior Product Owner should teach his people how to be effective investors.

Making a Case for a Scrum Program Owner

While the Scrum framework defines no role above that of Product Owner, a case can be made for a role that accepts accountability for making investment decisions for families of products. This role might be called Scrum Program Owner.

A Scrum Product Owner invests the resources he or she has been given in order to maximize the return on that investment. The goal is to produce the most valuable product it is possible to make using those resources.

One question the Scrum framework does not address, though, is how to determine how many resources to give a Product Owner to use. Both single-team and scaled Scrum variants allow for small and large numbers of developers to work on individual products. Who should be accountable for deciding how many developers to authorize for one product versus another?

The Product Owner for a single product should not be the one to decide how to allocate developers among multiple products. A single Product Owner is only accountable for the value of his or her product. Resource allocation decisions should be made by someone who is accountable for the value of all the products that are affected.

As an Agile Coach, you might coach the senior Product Owner to accept such a responsibility. He could play a valuable role in deciding which products in his "program" deserve the highest level of investment during any given Sprint. In effect, he would accept responsibility for maximizing the value of the family of products owned by the Product Owners under his management.

The Scrum Program Owner's role would be to make investment decisions for a group of products, just as a Product Owner makes investment decisions for an individual product. A Scrum Program Owner decides how many resources to invest in a product, whether it is a team of three people or a team of 300 people. Once again, the Scrum Program Owner's success would be measured based on the return on the investments made. His or her goal would be to maximize the total value of a family of products as opposed to the value of a single product.

Conclusion

As an Agile Coach, you propose that the senior Product Owner assume responsibility for allocating developer head counts between the company's different products. The senior Product Owner can choose to invest more heads in one product and fewer in another to maximize the value of the entire product family.

You can also coach the senior Product Owner to develop and teach techniques for estimating the potential value of various product improvements, and for measuring their actual value once they are implemented.

The senior Product Owner can accept accountability for the value of the entire product family, and his success can be measured by the return on investment realized by the entire product family.

Case 14:

Coaching a Spineless Product Owner

You are a Scrum Master joining an existing team. The Product Owner seems to be hesitant to make any decisions. He takes his priorities from the C-level road map release document that is produced each quarter. He uses the team's business analyst to write the Product Backlog items based on the road map. He doesn't really care which Product Backlog items the developers choose to accept into their Sprints in each Sprint Planning meeting.

When someone asks about priorities, he shrugs his shoulders and says, "I'm just following the road map." When someone asks about the progress of the product, he just says, "I don't know, it is up to the developers."

Your assignment:

1. Analyze the situation vis-à-vis the Scrum framework.
2. Come up with a plan of action to address problems with the team, if any.

This case illustrates some of the common issues that arise when a Product Owner is unable to accept accountability for the value of a product.

Initial Analysis

In every product development effort, there are always two decisions to make: what to develop and how to develop it. The Scrum framework is designed to allocate decision-making responsibility to people competent to make the necessary choices.

In exchange, the Scrum framework holds those people accountable for the results of those choices.

The Scrum framework gives a Product Owner authority to make all decisions related to what the Scrum Team should make. The Product Owner's responsibility is to maximize the value of the Scrum Team's work product.

In this case study, there is a Product Owner who disclaims all responsibility. The Product Owner makes no decisions about what should be created or how it should be prioritized. He makes no effort to guide the product's development toward results that maximize its value. He accepts the priorities implied by the C-level road map and accepts the choices the development team has made regarding what they will work on during each Sprint. He does these things so that he can avoid accountability. He does them so that no one can blame him for making a wrong decision.

Since no one is making decisions about maximizing the value of the product, this Scrum Team is currently operating without a Product Owner. Someone may claim to have this title, but the functions of product ownership are missing. The main responsibility of product ownership is to make sure the Scrum Team is producing value. If no one shoulders that responsibility, the ability of the Scrum Team to produce value will suffer.

Why Is There No Product Owner?

As Scrum Master, you decide to investigate the situation. You want to find out why the Product Owner is reluctant to make any decisions. The inability to take responsibility may not be the problem, but rather, a symptom of an underlying dysfunction. It is important to understand why product ownership is missing, even though an individual with the title "Product Owner" is on the team.

In the Scrum framework, a product is something that can be produced and that has an objectively measurable value. A product must have a value that can be measured, because the Scrum framework's purpose is to create valuable products. The Product Owner's job is to maximize the value of the product he or she owns. It is impossible to maximize something that cannot be measured. The value of a product must be measurable or else it is impossible to decide how to increase its value.

What Does This Product Owner Actually Own?

The first question to ask is what does the Product Owner own. The second question to ask is whether the product the Scrum Team is working on is even a product at all. One explanation for the lack of product ownership here might be that there is no product to own.

In this case study, the product the Scrum Team is working on is a middleware set of application programming interfaces (APIs) that sit between customer-facing smartphone apps and a back-end transaction processing engine. The company is a financial services provider that allows its customers to perform several different types of financial transactions using the smartphone apps. The apps capture requests and send them to the back-end engine through the API layer your team develops and maintains.

The road map the Product Owner claims to be following identifies a number of initiatives that are meant to produce new types of financial services to offer the company's customers. Each new service requires changes to the smartphone app software, changes to the back-end transaction processing engine, and changes to the API layer your team is assigned to develop. The road map describes a development timetable intended to synchronize the work of the different teams assigned to each application layer so that everything will be ready when it is time to release the new service.

Is it possible to measure the value of the middleware layer the Scrum Team is developing?

A product can be profitable for a company in three ways: by increasing its revenue, decreasing its costs, or decreasing its risk. If a new innovation produces a product that sells one million units at $2.99 apiece, that innovation increases revenue by $2.99 million. If a new innovation allows a company to sell one million units of a product for $1 less the cost per piece than before, the innovation's value is $1 million. If a new innovation eliminates a condition that has caused, on average, $1.5 million in losses per year, that innovation has a value of $1.5 million per year.

Can a middleware layer increase revenue? No. It can only support new services that increase revenue by coordinating with the customer-facing and back-end layers. It cannot increase revenue directly itself.

Can a middleware layer decrease cost? No. Again, it can only support cost-saving initiatives by coordinating with the other layers involved.

Can a middleware layer decrease risk? Once again, no, it cannot.

As Scrum Master, you determine that there is no way to measure the value of the API middleware layer objectively. This means there is no way to maximize its value. There are no decisions a Product Owner can make that would affect its value.

The API middleware layer is not a product. There is nothing for the Product Owner to own.

What Is the Actual Product and Who Owns It?

The Scrum Teams in this company are organized around functional layers. One layer is the customer-facing app layer; another is the API middleware layer, and the third is the back-end transaction processing layer.

None of these layers is a product. None of them has values that can be measured objectively. None of them can be sold.

What does the company sell? Financial services. Those services are the company's products. Each service is a product a Product Owner can own. Each service is a product a Scrum Team (or a set of Scrum Teams) can develop in order to increase its value. Each service has a value that can be measured directly.

You note that the C-level road map is a timetable for producing a set of new financial services to offer the marketplace. Those new services are the products that are to be produced. Each new service should have a Product Owner responsible for maximizing its value. Each new service should also have one or more teams accountable for creating it and delivering its value.

You realize the current model for aligning Scrum Teams with application layers has to change. Scrum Teams should be aligned with products, not layers. They should be measured and evaluated based on the value they create. They should be guided by Product Owners who are accountable for the measured value of the products they own. Things are very disorganized now. They need to be completely reorganized before any progress can be made.

Identifying the Real Product Owners

In the Scrum framework, the Product Owner has unlimited authority to shape the development of the product. In exchange, he or she accepts unlimited accountability for the value of the product that is owned. He or she is an investor, investing the time and resources of the development team (or teams) working on the product. The relative success of the Product Owner can be measured by the return on the investment (ROI) realized.

The decisions a Product Owner makes are the same kinds of decisions the C-level people made when creating the annual product development road map. They made decisions about investing millions of dollars in order to realize millions of dollars' worth of gains. Each new service described in the road map had a champion who believed in its potential and convinced the others to have it included. These champions had visions of the business opportunities the new services offered, and they had the organizational authority to get them included in the annual plan.

You realize the real Product Owners are not the ones working at the team level. The real Product Owners are those champions at the C level who have both the product vision and the authority to get their products included in the road map. They have expressed their visions of the developed products by creating a waterfall-style road map. You decide you need to teach and coach them to express their visions by creating Scrum framework Product Backlogs.

Realigning the Scrum Teams

Scrum framework development teams must have two characteristics. First, they must be cross-functional. This means they must be able to create the product themselves without depending on the help of anyone outside the team. They must be cross-functional because they must be able to accept accountability. A team cannot be accountable for creating a product if they do not have the ability to create it.

The second characteristic is that the team must be self-managing. This means they must make their own plans and their own decisions about how to create the product. They must have unlimited authority to answer the question “How should we make it?” with no one outside the team being able to contradict them.

The reason the team must be self-managing is again about accountability. A team cannot be accountable for its results unless it makes its own decisions. If someone tells the team members what to do and how to do it, they have no ownership of the outcome of those decisions.

After you have coached the C-level champions into creating Product Backlogs for the new financial services they wish to create, you place the Product Backlogs before the developers who have been working on the various “layer” teams. You ask the developers to organize themselves into teams with the necessary skills to work though and deliver items in each Product Backlog.

Once the developers have picked the products they wish to work on, you arrange for them to meet with the C-level product champions who own the products they have chosen. You encourage the developers and the champions to discuss and refine the items in the Product Backlogs.

Once the champions and the developers agree that at least a few of the most important needs make sense from a development point of view, they are ready to start their first Sprint.

How Big Should the Development Teams Be?

The Scrum framework advises that individual Scrum Teams should have no more than 10 developers each. This advice is meant to make sure development teams are not so large that they have difficulty managing themselves and their work.

Theoretically, a single Scrum Team can create any product, given enough time. It can do so by changing its membership as the product's technical needs change. Often, the time required for a single team to create a large or complicated product can be prohibitive. It can make good business sense to speed up the process by having more than 10 people work on the task.

The number of people to assign to developing a product is a business decision rather than a technical one. It is an investment decision that balances the cost of the people against the value they can create. Ultimately, it is a decision for the Product Owner to make, in consultation with the developers working on the product. The developers identify options for the number and kinds of people to add to the team. The Product Owner selects an option he or she feels will bring the best return.

In the end, each product must have a group of developers assigned to it who are cross-functional. They together must have all the skills and competencies necessary to turn the items in the Product Backlogs into valuable Increments.

In this case study, the Scrum Team for each product must have people who can deal with the user-facing apps, the API middleware, and the back-end transaction engine. All three skills are required to create a new financial service, and creating new services is the only way to create measurable value.

What About Scaled Scrum?

Sometimes the number of developers working on a product exceeds the recommended size of a single development team. Generally speaking, the smaller a team is, the better. A small group of people can understand what everyone is doing and can step in to help individual members when necessary. A large group might have trouble keeping track of what is going on within it and might spend a lot of time just understanding its status. Scrum Teams must manage themselves, and large teams make that difficult.

In this case study, one of the new services is a small one that only merits an investment of a single Scrum development team to produce. You teach and coach the formation of a development team for it and get them started on a normal Sprint schedule.

Two other new services represent much better opportunities and merit the investment of 20 people and 35 people, respectively. You facilitate the formation of a group of 20 cross-functional people for one service and a group of 35 cross-functional people for the other service. Then you teach and coach them to organize themselves to divide the work in ways that make sense.

During the Sprint Planning meeting for each product, you teach and coach the Product Owner to negotiate with each group of developers which Product Backlog items will be selected for delivery. All 20 of the developers for one product negotiate with its Product Owner, and all 35 of the developers for the other product negotiate with its Product Owner. Once agreement is reached on the set of Product Backlog items to be delivered, the Product Owners leave. The 20 developers break into teams of 10 or fewer people to tackle individual Product Backlog items they selected as a group; the 35 developers do the same. They all start their Sprint. In addition to the normal Sprint activities, they also keep track of any dependencies that might exist between their teams and take steps to make sure they are resolved.

When the Scrum framework is used by more than one Scrum Team to create a product, it is called scaled Scrum. There are several versions of scaled Scrum, including Nexus, Large Scale Scrum or LeSS, Disciplined Agile Development System or DADS, Scaled Agile Framework or SAFe, and Scrum@Scale.

You choose to teach and coach the use of something similar to Nexus and LeSS. The principal thrust of both approaches is to preserve the Scrum Team characteristics of cross-functionality and self-management. In single-team Scrum, the 10 or fewer people who make up the development team must have all the skills necessary to create the product and must break the work down into tasks that they track and manage themselves. In these two scaled Scrum frameworks, the larger development group must be cross-functional and must manage its own tasks. In addition, the group must break itself down into smaller subteams and coordinate the work of those subteams.

Conclusion

This Product Owner made no decisions because there was no product for him to own. No decision he made could make any difference. He avoided making decisions to avoid blame for results over which he had no control.

You identified the actual products that were being produced and identified the actual Product Owners who could be accountable for them. Then you taught and coached them to create Product Backlogs for the products.

Next, you helped developers form cross-functional, self-managing teams to create the products. You taught and coached them to work with the Product Owners to refine and understand the items in the Product Backlogs.

For the products that justified large development teams, you taught and coached the developers to accept accountability for developing the product as a group but to divide themselves into smaller teams in order to undertake the work.

Case 15:

Dealing with Unhappy Stakeholders

You are a Scrum Master. You and your team are conducting a Sprint Review and a few stakeholders are present.

One of the stakeholders is very unhappy. She says the team got everything wrong and wants to throw out the latest Increment and start over.

Another stakeholder is OK with the content of the latest Increment but is angry over how long it is taking to create the finished product. He tells the Product Owner that the team had better double their productivity or else funding will be cut.

A third stakeholder is upset about the sequence of the Product Backlog. She wants several low-priority items to be moved to a higher priority. She wants several of these features developed by the end of the next Sprint.

Tempers are starting to flare. All three stakeholders start shouting at the Product Owner and the team. The Product Owner starts to shout right back.

Your assignment:

1. Analyze this situation vis-à-vis the Scrum framework.
2. Formulate a strategy for dealing with this situation and outline the first few steps you will take.

This case illustrates some of the challenges and conflicts that are part of product ownership.

Initial Analysis

The company you are a part of recently underwent an Agile transformation. Outside consultants were brought in to teach everyone the fundamentals of Agile and the Scrum framework. Developers were organized into Scrum Teams oriented around creating specific products. Each product was assigned to a Product Owner who accepted accountability for increasing the value of the product (or products) they owned. So far, so good.

The transformation effort was sponsored by a group of three C-suite executives: the chief information officer (CIO), chief technology officer (CTO), and chief marketing officer (CMO).

They initiated and funded the project after the company suffered several high-profile software development failures. Three multimillion-dollar projects were organized according to the Project Management Institute's Software Development Life Cycle (SDLC) model. Each one had a timeline that stretched over two years, and each one ended up being many months late and significantly over budget. When the software was finally delivered, it was functionally obsolete. Almost the entire team of mid-level technical managers involved was let go as a result.

The CIO, CTO, and CMO brought in high-level management consultants for advice on what to do. The management consultants recommended abandoning the SDLC model and adopting an Agile-based approach. They said Agile practices make software developers much more efficient at developing and delivering results. They said dramatic improvements of up to 15 times better throughput could be realized.

The executives previously participated in the company's annual road map exercise. In this process, they and other C-suite participants discussed and set the development priorities that would govern the software development efforts for the coming year. The three failed projects had been conceived, prioritized, and funded through this process. The three executives were anxious to address the business needs represented by the failed endeavors, and they resolved to restart the projects using Agile practices. They were hopeful that the promised 15-fold increase in throughput would allow the projects to be completed quickly. They formally amended the year's road map and set aggressive deadlines for delivering results.

The Sprint Review described in this case study occurred after six Sprints had been completed. A lot of completed software had been delivered, but the results did not match the timeline called for in the amended road map. The three executives (the stakeholders) were reacting with a mixture of alarm, dismay, and panic. They feared that another multimillion-dollar fiasco was in the works and this time they would be the ones who would be terminated.

Applying the Scrum Framework

The Scrum framework recognizes that there are two kinds of decisions to be made when developing new products of any kind, not just software products: what to make and how to make it.

In Scrum, questions regarding how to make the product are given to the development team to answer. They are a group of technical people who together have the ability to create the product. They are given absolute authority to decide how the product is to be made. In exchange, they accept absolute accountability for making and delivering it.

Likewise, questions regarding what to make are given to a person who has the ability to answer the questions effectively. The person is given authority to set goals for the development team to work toward. In exchange, this person accepts accountability for the value of the results the development team delivers.

The person who answers the “what to make” questions is known as the Product Owner. His or her responsibility is to maximize the value of the product. He or she does so by identifying and prioritizing valuable additions and changes to be made to it.

At the beginning of every Sprint, the Product Owner negotiates with the development team to reach agreement on the specific changes and additions to be made. The Product Owner identifies the items that would be the most valuable to implement while the development team considers which ones would be practical to undertake.

The Product Owner acts as an investor. His or her job is to invest the time and talents of the development team in order to create a more valuable product. The time and talents of a development team can represent quite a bit of money, even for just a single Sprint. The Product Owner’s responsibility is to make sure the development team delivers more value than it costs to employ them to create that value.

Like any investor, the way to measure the effectiveness of a Product Owner is to consider the amount of value realized compared to the cost of realizing it. In other words, the Product Owner can be evaluated based on the return on investment (ROI) the Scrum Team delivers. The higher the ROI is, the better. A negative ROI is a good indication that a Product Owner does not know how to do the job.

Measuring Value

One of the most important principles within the Scrum framework is the principle of empiricism. Empiricism calls for decisions that are based on observations and measurements rather than opinions and/or predictions. Empiricism holds that no predictions can ever be regarded as certain. Certainty is only possible when measuring something that has already happened. The future cannot be measured. Only the past can be measured.

For this reason, the Scrum framework requires that all decisions be made based on measurements rather than predictions. For the Product Owner, this means decisions about maximizing the value of a product must be based on actual measurements of that value. For the Product Owner to do his or her job, he or she must find a way to measure the current value of the product. He or she must also measure how the product's value changes as a result of the development team's efforts.

A product can have measurable value in three principal ways.

1. By increasing revenue: If a new product is to be sold, the way to measure its value is to sell it. The value of the product is equal to the price a customer is willing to pay for it, multiplied by the number of customers willing to buy it.
2. By decreasing costs: If a product reduces the unit cost of a service by $1 and the company sells one million units per year, the value of such a product is $1 million per year.
3. By decreasing risk: If a certain risk exists that costs a company $1 million whenever things go south, and on average they go south once per year, eliminating this risk has a value of $1 million per year.

The value of any commercial product should be measured in terms of dollars and cents. Not everything that is valuable (such as friendship) can be measured in monetary terms, but commercial products must be. The reason is that the investments needed to create commercial products are measured in terms of money. The only way to calculate the return on such investments is to compare the monetary cost of the investment with the monetary value of the resultant product.

Like all investors, the Product Owner faces a bit of a conundrum. The Scrum framework calls for all decisions to be made based on measurements, but there is no certain way to measure the value of a product before it is created. That value can only be measured after the product exists. The Product Owner must speculate about the potential value of the product, then confirm the accuracy of that speculation after the product is delivered.

One way experienced Product Owners deal with this challenge is by making predictions about the value of small pieces of the product and checking them once they have been created. The Product Owner identifies small additions to the value of the product by adding them to the Product Backlog. The Product Backlog is a prioritized list of all the detailed needs the product is intended to fill. Each Sprint, the development team agrees to improve the product in order to fill some of those needs. If the Product Owner is doing his or her job properly, each need will have an estimated value that can be realized when it is filled. There will also be an indication about how that value can be measured.

The Scrum framework Product Owner often borrows a concept from the world of Lean product development. Lean emphasizes the importance of the minimum viable product, or MVP. When something new is being developed, Lean calls for getting a version of the product into the hands of customers as early in the process as possible. By creating a product with the minimum number of features necessary to be usable, it is possible to get early customer feedback on it in time to make adjustments in development plans.

The Scrum framework is designed to make it possible to get this kind of early feedback. The Scrum framework calls for the completion of a "done" improvement to the product each and every Sprint. For an improvement to be considered "done," it must be ready to give to a customer with no further work required.

The improvement must be “done” because only something that can be given to a customer can have any measurable value. How can the value of something that is not finished be measured? It cannot be sold. It cannot reduce any costs. It cannot reduce any risks. It may have potential value, but that value cannot be realized until it is complete with no further work required.

The Product Owner should identify and prioritize the items in the Product Backlog with an eye on getting functionality into the hands of customers as early as possible. The Product Owner should keep the idea of an MVP in mind. The sooner a part of the product can be put to use, the sooner its value can be measured. Once that value has been measured, the value can give feedback to the Product Owner to guide future decisions.

Product Owners Versus Stakeholders

Getting back to our Sprint Review, it is important to realize the inherent differences between Product Owners and stakeholders. Both may have considerable power and authority. The Product Owner, however, accepts personal accountability for the value of the product he or she owns. Stakeholders do not.

A Product Owner can only accept accountability for the product if he or she has absolute authority to define and prioritize the way it is developed. If a Product Owner has to get permission to add something to the Product Backlog, or if a stakeholder can overrule the Product Owner’s decisions, the Product Owner is not a Product Owner at all. The Product Owner cannot be held accountable for the results of someone else’s decisions. If a stakeholder tries to tell the Product Owner what he or she should do about the product's development, he or she should tell the stakeholder "no."

During this Sprint Review, that is exactly what happened. All three stakeholders demanded that the Product Owner make changes the Product Owner didn't agree with. He told them "no." Tempers flared and a loud argument ensued.

What Should the Scrum Master Do?

A Scrum framework Scrum Master is a teacher and a coach. His or her job is to teach everyone involved how the Scrum framework works and coach them to use its tools properly.

As the Scrum Master, one thing you can do is turn the conversation away from what *should* be done and toward what *has* been done. Differences about what should be done involve differences of opinion and/or predictions of results. Talking about what has happened turns the discussion toward considering measurable facts. People can agree on facts even if they disagree about opinions.

The fundamental fear the stakeholders are expressing is that the current project might result in another fiasco. They are worried that more time and more millions of dollars will be wasted. They are worried because the course of development is not adhering to the plan set out in the company's annual road map. They made the road map based on the assumption that Agile would make the developers 15 times more productive than before. Not only have the road map's milestones not been met, but many of the features delivered thus far do not even appear in their plan.

The best way to address the stakeholders' fear that time and money is being wasted is to point to the measured value of the features that have been delivered so far.

The Product Owner has done a good job getting product improvements into the hands of customers quickly. Those customers have provided valuable feedback. As a result, the measured value of the improvements delivered so far actually exceeds the estimates the Product Owner used to prioritize the work.

Even more important, the customers helped the Product Owner understand that several proposed major improvements would actually have little value in their eyes. That is one reason some of the milestones in the road map have been skipped. If the Product Owner had prioritized them and the developers had implemented them, all of that time and money would have been wasted. It would have cost a lot and produced very little value.

By keeping in close contact with customers, the Product Owner has gotten a much better idea about how to understand the potential value of the various items in the Product Backlog. After six Sprints, he feels confident his speculation about an item's value will be pretty close to its actual value once the item has been created. True, his estimates are guesses, but they are educated guesses based on the measured value of product improvements that have already been delivered.

So how should you and the Product Owner handle the situation?

One of the stakeholders claimed the developers got everything wrong and said the latest Increment should be thrown out. One thing that either the Product Owner or you, as the Scrum Master, can do is to suggest that they measure the value of the Increment. The value is measured by giving the item to the customers to evaluate. Let them decide whether the developers got everything wrong or not. Let their feedback determine whether the improvement should be thrown out.

Another stakeholder is angry about how long it is taking for the development team to deliver. He demands that productivity be doubled or else funding will be cut. He is angry because he was led to believe that an Agile approach would increase productivity 15-fold. He expects to see that kind of improvement.

One thing the Product Owner can do to address this is compare the cost of running the team to the amount of value that has been delivered. He can point out that results must be measured in terms of value delivered, rather than whether arbitrary milestones have been met. He can point out that measurements indicate that, so far, the efforts of the development team have returned 15 times as much value as it has cost to run the six Sprints that have been completed. Using the Scrum framework did not result in development timelines that were 15 times shorter. It resulted in the delivery of improvements that were 15 times more valueable than they cost.

The third stakeholder demanded that the order of the Product Backlog be changed and that several low-priority items be included in the next Sprint. She feels these low-priority items should be high-priority items.

The Product Owner can counter this by explaining that priorities in the Product Backlog are set based on his estimate of their value and confirmed by feedback from customers. The Product Owner has talked with customers about their needs and feels that other items will yield more value if they are implemented first. The Product Owner can point to the estimates he gave for prior Product Backlog items and compare those estimates to the actual value the improvements had when they were complete and measured. Comparing those estimates to the actual measured values of the improvements can give the Product Owner confidence that his prioritization choices are correct. He can then invite the stakeholder to review the measurements and point out any mistakes he might have made.

Conclusion

Generally, it is impossible to reconcile differences of opinion. Often, those differences are resolved based on the organizational power or authority of the people involved. Higher-ranking people can and do overrule lower-ranking people. This does not settle any differences. It only causes the more powerful person's opinion to prevail.

The Scrum framework does not rely on opinions. It emphasizes measured facts. Unlike differences of opinion, it is very possible to resolve differences in the understanding of facts. The key is the principle of transparency. Transparency means that all the key information about the product and the work being performed is visible and accessible to everyone concerned. As long as everyone can see and use the same set of facts, it is possible for them to evaluate those facts and come to the same set of conclusions.

Summary

The Scrum framework is an exceptionally powerful tool for organizing the creation of valuable products. Since it was first presented in 1995, it has grown to become the most widely used framework in the software development industry.

It might also be said that Scrum is the most widely misused framework in the software development industry. Many organizations believe they are using Scrum when in fact they are only using certain parts of it. They embrace its more understandable pieces and omit the less-intuitive ones. Often, they find that the results are unsatisfactory. This can (and does) lead many to conclude that using Scrum is merely a fad that is destined to fade away over time.

The Scrum framework is a response to the fact that solving complex problems requires a process of discovery. Solutions to complex problems must be discovered rather than planned.

The Software Development Life Cycle (SDLC or waterfall) approach involves creating a step-by-step plan for constructing a product. This plan is similar to a recipe. Follow the steps, add the right ingredients, and you will get the result you want. (And if you do not get the result you want, the implication is that you did not follow the recipe properly.)

The Scrum framework and its creators eschew the use of recipes when creating new products. It is ironic to notice, then, that the Scrum framework itself is a recipe. It is a list of ingredients and instructions on how to combine them.

Many people attempt to follow this recipe, but they often leave out ingredients they do not understand. The results are often unsatisfactory.

Before choosing to leave out parts of the Scrum recipe (or add new ones), it is advisable to understand the purpose of those parts. It is important to understand why those parts are there. It is important to understand not how the Scrum framework works, but why it works.

When you take away all the "clutter," the Scrum framework turns out to be very simple.

1. Decisions about what to make must be made by people who are competent to make them and can be held accountable for the results.
2. Decisions about how to make those things must be made by people who are competent to make them and can be held accountable for the results.
3. Decisions should be made based on measurements rather than guesses or predictions.
4. Measurable results should be generated (and measured) frequently.
5. Only a few simple tools are necessary to manage the process.

The 15 case studies in this book involved bringing those situations back in line with these five principles.

Rather than trying to follow the Scrum recipe exactly, the Scrum professional is advised to always keep these five principles in mind. Going through the motions of the Scrum framework without the necessary authorities, accountabilities, and measurements in place is a recipe for disaster. Altering or omitting specific parts of the Scrum recipe while preserving these principles will bring all the benefits that have made the Scrum framework famous.

Scrum is a simple framework for empowering people to make decisions, own the consequences of those decisions, and create awesome results.

Index:

- Acceptance Test Driven Development: 54
- Agile: 7, 8, 10, 11, 12, 13, 19, 20, 23, 24, 30, 33, 49, 62, 153, 156, 163, 164, 165, 166, 169, 171, 172, 181, 184, 185, 190, 192
- Agile Manifesto: 11
- Agile MBA: 11
- Agile metrics: 153, 156
- Agile Transformation: 7, 13, 23
- Amazon Web Services: 72
- Angel investor: 121
- ATDD: 54
- BDD: 54
- Behavior Driven Development: 54
- big data: 35
- Big Room meeting: 78, 79
- business analysts: 26, 27
- CIO: 8, 23, 30, 117, 184
- command and control: 141
- COVID-19: 12, 153, 156, 159
- cross-functionality: 37, 80, 82, 91, 182
- CSP: 14
- daily bug report: 51
- Daily Scrum: 19, 35, 36, 37, 44, 77, 79, 89, 93, 143, 144
- Definition of Done: 54, 95, 147, 148
- delivering value: 25, 46, 76, 91, 94, 110, 145, 146, 170
- dependencies: 73, 77, 78, 79, 80, 86, 87, 89, 91, 118, 158, 160, 181
- DevOps: 76, 77, 78, 80
- differences of opinion: 190, 193
- e-commerce website: 81
- elephants in the room: 100
- empirical process control: 61

- Empiricism: 186
- engineering manager: 47, 48, 49
- forecasts: 35, 127
- Increment: 18, 48, 50, 51, 52, 54, 55, 59, 78, 79, 101, 180, 183, 191
- iteration: 124
- Java: 7, 13, 66, 85, 93, 94, 95, 96, 97, 98, 99, 101, 102, 103, 104
- Ken Schwaber: 15
- lead developers: 37, 38
- legacy big iron: 23, 30
- LeSS: 110, 181, 182
- management by walking around: 154
- maximizing value: 32, 167
- measure work: 65
- measuring value: 162
- MySQL: 72
- Navigating Hybrid Scrum Environments: 8, 14
- Nexus: 77, 78, 80, 110, 181, 182
- offshore: 47, 49, 81, 82, 85, 91
- pair programming: 55, 56
- planning poker: 36
- prioritization: 192
- Product Backlog: 17, 18, 19, 27, 28, 29, 30, 31, 32, 34, 35, 36, 38, 39, 40, 41, 42, 43, 45, 46, 51, 52, 53, 54, 55, 59, 60, 61, 63, 64, 66, 68, 69, 77, 78, 79, 83, 84, 86, 87, 88, 89, 90, 93, 95, 96, 102, 103, 108, 109, 110, 111, 112, 113, 114, 122, 123, 124, 125, 126, 127, 133, 134, 135, 136, 137, 139, 146, 147, 148, 149, 150, 156, 157, 158, 159, 160, 163, 165, 173, 178, 179, 180, 181, 182, 183, 188, 189, 191, 192
- Product Backlog refinement: 39, 43, 46, 64, 68, 77, 86, 88, 136, 137
- Product Owner: 7, 14, 16, 17, 18, 19, 25, 26, 27, 28, 29, 30, 31, 32, 33, 34, 35, 36, 38, 39, 40, 42, 43, 44, 45, 47, 48, 51, 52, 53, 54, 55, 59, 60, 61, 63, 64, 66, 68, 74, 75,

76, 78, 79, 82, 83, 84, 86, 87, 89, 90, 93, 94, 95, 97, 100, 101, 102, 103, 108, 109, 110, 111, 112, 113, 115, 122, 123, 124, 125, 126, 129, 133, 139, 146, 148, 149, 150, 151, 157, 158, 160, 163, 164, 165, 166, 167, 168, 169, 170, 171, 172, 173, 174, 175, 176, 177, 178, 180, 181, 182, 183, 184, 186, 187, 188, 189, 190, 191, 192

- PSM II: 8, 14, 15
- PSM III: 8, 15
- return on investment (ROI): 65, 186
- road map: 117, 118, 119, 120, 121, 122, 123, 127, 142, 143, 145, 147, 148, 149, 173, 174, 175, 177, 178, 184, 185, 190, 191
- SAFe: 110, 181
- Scaled Scrum: 86, 180
- Scrum events: 35, 82, 141, 143
- Scrum Master: 8, 14, 17, 19, 35, 36, 38, 39, 43, 47, 48, 54, 59, 68, 71, 81, 93, 100, 105, 108, 110, 117, 122, 123, 127, 141, 142, 143, 148, 163, 164, 167, 169, 173, 174, 176, 183, 190, 191
- Scrum Program Owner: 170, 171
- Scrum roles: 82
- Scrum@Scale: 110, 181
- SDLC: 184, 195
- self-management: 37, 94, 104, 158, 182
- Silicon Valley Professional Scrum: 10, 12, 13, 15
- Software Development Life Cycle: 184, 195
- Sprint: 17, 18, 19, 32, 34, 35, 36, 37, 38, 39, 42, 43, 44, 45, 47, 50, 51, 52, 53, 54, 55, 56, 59, 60, 61, 62, 63, 64, 66, 67, 68, 69, 71, 77, 78, 79, 80, 85, 86, 87, 88, 89, 90, 93, 95, 96, 100, 101, 102, 103, 112, 113, 122, 124, 125, 126, 133, 137, 138, 139, 141, 143, 144, 146, 147, 150, 151, 163, 168, 169, 170, 171, 173, 174, 179, 181, 183, 185, 186, 188, 189, 190, 191, 192
- Sprint Backlog: 17, 18, 51, 53, 69, 77, 79, 89, 102
- Sprint Goal: 43
- Sprint Planning Meeting: 18, 42

- Sprint Retrospective: 19, 35, 38, 45, 50, 71, 90, 93, 100, 101, 102, 103, 113, 144, 146
- Sprint Review: 19, 32, 35, 44, 45, 85, 87, 89, 90, 93, 101, 113, 138, 139, 144, 146, 183, 185, 189, 190
- SQL: 66, 71, 72, 73, 74, 79
- stakeholders: 119, 120, 155, 156, 160, 183, 185, 189, 190, 191
- stored procedures: 71, 72, 73, 74
- story points: 35, 59, 60, 62, 68, 126, 163, 164, 165
- T-shirt sizes: 63
- TDD: 54
- technical debt: 147, 165
- technical specifications: 26, 28
- the COVID-19 crisis: 159
- The Job Hackers: 11
- time zone difference: 74
- top management: 25, 32, 33, 118, 142, 143, 148, 149
- transparency: 17, 100, 193
- user story: 28, 29, 36, 40, 87
- user story format: 28, 29, 36, 87
- velocity: 59, 60, 126, 134, 163, 164
- vice president of sales: 129, 133, 137, 138
- waterfall: 23, 24, 33, 118, 121, 122, 132, 133, 164, 166, 167, 178, 195
- website development: 82, 84
- XML: 88, 89

Made in United States
North Haven, CT
04 November 2026

21771705R00118